*Designing water supply and sanitation projects
to meet demand in rural and peri-urban communities*

Book 1:
Concept, Principles and Practice

Designing water supply and sanitation projects to meet demand in rural and peri-urban communities

Book 1.
Concept, Principles and Practice

Paul Deverill, Simon Bibby,
Alison Wedgwood & Ian Smout

Water, Engineering and Development Centre
Loughborough University
2002

WEDC

Water, Engineering and Development Centre,
Loughborough University,
Leicestershire, LE11 3TU, UK

A reference copy of this publication is also available online at:
http://www.lboro.ac.uk/wedc/projects/d4d.htm

Deverill P., Bibby S., Wedgwood A. & Smout I. (2002)
Designing water supply and sanitation projects to meet demand
in rural and peri-urban communities
Book 1: Concept, Principles and Practice
WEDC, Loughborough University, UK.

ISBN 13 Paperback: 9781843800064
ISBN Library Ebook: 9781788532877
Book DOI: http://dx.doi.org/10.3362/99781788532877

A catalogue record for this book is available from the British Library.

This document is an output from a project funded by the UK
Department for International Development (DFID)
for the benefit of low-income countries.
The views expressed are not necessarily those of DFID or the other organisations who
contributed to the development of these guidelines.

Designed and produced at WEDC

This edition is reprinted and distributed by Practical Action Publishing.
Since 1974, Practical Action Publishing has published and disseminated books and information
in support of international development work throughout the world. Practical Action
Publishing trades only in support of its parent charity objectives and any profits are covenanted
back to Practical Action (Charity Reg. No. 247257, Group VAT Registration No. 880 9924 76).

Cover photographs:
Top left: Partners in Development cc (South Africa)
Top right: John Holmes/WaterAid (Nepal)
Bottom left: Sohrab Baghri/WEDC
Bottom right: Partners in Development cc (South Africa)

Acknowledgements

The financial support of the Department for International Development of the British Government is gratefully acknowledged. The authors would also like to thank the many organisations and individuals that have contributed to the development of these guidelines, without whose interest and participation this work could not have been undertaken.

South Africa
The Mvula Trust

Department of Water Affairs and Forestry, Pretoria

Partners in Development cc, Pietermaritzburg

Watsup Development, Johannesburg

India
UNICEF WES; New Delhi, Orissa and Madhya Pradesh

Rural Water Supply and Sanitation Department, Ganjam District, Orissa

United Artists Association, Ganjam District, Orissa

Mike Webster, Water and Sanitation Programme, New Delhi

Nepal
Nepal Water for Health (NEWAH)

Department of Water Supply and Sewerage, Kathmandu

Rural Water Supply and Sanitation Fund Development Board, Kathmandu

UNICEF WES, Kathmandu

Gurkha Welfare Scheme, Pokhara

Self Reliant Drinking Water Support Programme, Pokhara

Rural Water Supply and Sanitation Support Program, Butwal

Lumanti, Kathmandu

Greg Whiteside

Tanzania
Oxfam (GB); Dar es Salaam and Shinyanga

WaterAid; Dar es Salaam and Dodoma

Concern Worldwide, Dar es Salaam

WAMMA, Dodoma

Finally, the authors wish to acknowledge Kevin Sansom and Sue Coates for their inputs and suggestions, and the patience and skills of Glenda McMahon of the WEDC Publications Office.

Who should read this booklet?

This book has been specifically written for *practitioners* responsible for implementing water supply and sanitation projects in rural and peri-urban areas.

Practitioners include engineers and technical staff, social facilitators, financial and gender specialists and project managers, with different roles and responsibilities within the project framework. In order to be able to use 'demand', it is essential that individuals work as in a multidisciplinary team - together with the communities involved. The concept of meeting demand does not belong to any particular profession.

How to use this booklet

The objective of this book is to develop an understanding of what is a fairly complex issue. As far as possible, jargon has been avoided. The glossary helps explain some of the terminology used.

The information provided in Part II also includes a number of practical tools and checklists. These can be extracted and adapted to enhance an existing strategy, taking into account the local situation and the capacity available.

Contents

Abbreviations

AF	Annuity factor
CVM	Contingent valuation methodology (see glossary).
DFID	Department for International Development (UK)
DWAF	Department for Water Affairs and Forestry (South Africa)
ERM	Environmental Resources Management Ltd (UK)
GTZ	Gesellschaft für Technische Zusammenarbeit (German Federal aid agency)
IIED	International Institute for the Environment and Development (UK)
M&E	Monitoring and evaluation
NEWAH	Nepal Water for Health
NGO	Non Governmental Organisation
O&M	Operation and maintenance
pcd	per capita day (per person per day)
PHAST	Participatory Hygiene and Sanitation Transformation (see glossary)
PREPP	Participation, Ranking, Experience, Perceptions and Partnership (see glossary)
SL	Sustainable Livelihoods
SWOC	Strengths, weaknesses, opportunities and constraints
UNICEF WES	United Nations Children's Fund/Water and Environmental Sanitation Programme
VIP	Ventilated Improved Pit Latrine
WEDC	Water, Engineering and Development Centre (UK)
WHO	World Health Organisation
WSSCC	Water Supply and Sanitation Collaborative Council

*Designing water supply and sanitation projects
to meet demand in rural and peri-urban communities*

Part I:
Concept and Principles

"The freedom to make and continue making choices is perhaps the greatest single index of well being"

Opening line of Professor Tom Kirkwood's 4th Reith Lecture,
25th April 2001

Concept and Principles: Summary

The principal lesson from the International Drinking Water and Sanitation Decade was that *progress and continuing success depend most on responding to consumer demand*[1]. Other evaluations have concluded that water supply and sanitation systems that have not met demand have problems of under-use, poor maintenance and poor cost recovery.

Despite the considerable achievements of the water supply and sanitation sector, a change in strategy is needed to improve the use and sustainability of the services provided - one that recognises the fundamental importance of user demand.

Defining demand

In these guidelines, demand is defined as *an informed expression of desire for a particular service, assessed by the investments people are prepared to make, over the lifetime of the service, to receive and sustain it*. These investments may consist of financial and economic resources as well as the time and interest that users are prepared to commit.

The definition enables demand to be used as a practical tool to guide project design. It is important to understand what this implies:

■ People should make key decisions about the services they are to receive. To do this, they must be informed about the complications of the choices they make.

■ Demand reflects individual perceptions and priorities, many of which are expressed at household level. To meet demand, projects need to focus on households as well as communities, taking into account the different demands of men and women.

■ Meeting the demand of some users for higher levels of service may result in others being deprived. This may discriminate against those less able to articulate their demands unless precautions are taken.

■ The poorest people in society have very limited access to the resources that could be used to indicate demand. What little they have may be fully committed as part of a day to day survival strategy. A welfare approach may still be needed to ensure the most vulnerable in a community are not excluded.

These points reinforce the importance of using a number of appropriate indicators to measure demand at different stages of the project process.

Meeting demand

Demand is met by enabling people to choose their preferred service from a range of feasible options. Collective decision making is required when individual choice is not practical. The final form the service takes will often emerge through negotiation, reflecting social, technical, environmental, financial and institutional constraints.

For project staff, a key challenge is to identify, develop, cost, test and communicate feasible options which have the potential to meet demand. This process is guided by *demand assessment*, for which a variety of techniques can be used.

In some cases, demand must be *stimulated* before it can be responded to. This situation is often encountered when sanitation improvements are being considered. Such situations pose a number of challenges to project staff. Modifying people's perceptions requires very different skills to those needed to implement a water supply project, and can also take a great deal of time.

In practical terms, hidden or latent demand may be stimulated by promoting options with characteristics that people find desirable, at a price they are willing to pay. The technique, is known as social marketing.

Enhancing an existing approach

It is recommended that the demand 'factor' is incorporated into an existing approach, improving its impact and sustainability. The extent that this can be done largely depends on the capacity and resources available and the project's policy, institutional and legal environment. Nevertheless, in most cases there is considerable potential for an implementing organisation to develop an appropriate, demand responsive project strategy. The eight guiding principles of meeting demand that conclude Part I provide a framework for change.

1: Cairncross (1992)

1. Background

The principal lesson from the International Drinking Water and Sanitation Decade, according to Cairncross (1992), was that "progress and continuing success depend most on responding to consumer demand". Other evaluations have concluded that water and sanitation systems that have not met demand have problems of under use, poor maintenance and poor cost recovery.

Such findings have resulted in the emergence of a number of demand responsive or demand driven approaches. Whilst these are now being implemented and, in some cases, scaled up, it is too early to say how effective they will be in terms of their longer-term impact and sustainability.

Meanwhile, differing opinions of what demand is, and how it can be expressed and assessed, have fuelled a largely ideological debate. Attention has been rightly focused on the potentially negative impact that demand responsive approaches may have on those least able to express their demands.

Irrespective of this legitimate concern, one fact is clear. After several decades of consolidated development effort and billions of dollars of investment in water supply and sanitation, a great deal remains to be done (see Box 1.1). Despite the considerable achievements in both practice and policy in the water supply and sanitation sector, more is needed to improve the sustainability and use of the services being provided.

Demand for water supply and sanitation should be seen in this context. First of all, we need to understand what we mean by "demand". This is particularly relevant when one considers that the majority of those without access to improved water supplies and sanitation are the poor who may find it difficult to voice their demand.

Box 1.1.   The global situation: water supply and sanitation

"At the beginning of 2000 one-sixth (1.1 billion people) of the world's population was without access to improved water supply and two-fifths (2.4 billion people) lacked access to improved sanitation. The majority of these people live in Asia and Africa. Fewer than one-half of all Asians have access to improved sanitation and two out of five Africans lack improved water supply.

Moreover, rural services still lag far behind urban services. Sanitation coverage in rural areas, for example, is less than half that in urban settings, even though 80% of those lacking adequate sanitation (2 billion people) live in rural areas – some 1.3 billion in China and India alone.

These figures are all the more shocking because they reflect the results of at least twenty years of concerted effort and publicity to improve coverage".

WHO (2000)

2. Perceptions of demand

The concept of being able to respond to user demand is made more complicated by the differing perceptions of what is meant by demand. These tend to reflect the profession and ideology of the person concerned.

2.1 Demand as a technical design parameter

Many engineers and technicians use 'demand', or more specifically *water demand,* to describe the quantity and quality of water that users consume or are expected to consume. This is associated with the level of service to be provided.

Level of service or service?

The term **level of service** (or service level) is used to describe the quality of the service being provided to users. This is often associated with physical infrastructure, for example, a communal tap, a yard tap, or an in-house private connection.

The word **service** has a more general significance, as it not only takes into account service levels, but also how these are managed and sustained.

Water demand is an important technical design parameter. It can be measured (for an existing water supply) or calculated using local data or, more typically, established norms and standards. Such calculations also take into account the number and type of users to be served, the anticipated population growth rate and the expected life span of the infrastructure being provided. It is also important to take into account the seasonal influence on water demand. This can be considerable, especially in rural areas where water is used to support people's livelihoods.

The influence price has on consumption is often not considered by technical staff, other than by applying an assumed rule which suggests that users are able to afford between 3% and 5% of their income to sustain a basic service. Apart from the difficulties of establishing household income and the fact that it may vary significantly from household to household, the rule has been discredited[1].

In practice, the impact and sustainability of a water supply scheme may be compromised because actual consumption is significantly more (or less) than the anticipated water demand. For example, people may want to use water for a variety of productive uses. This may lead to communal standpipes being 'upgraded' with hosepipes. In other cases, households may switch to traditional supplies when water is widely available.

2.2 Demand and willingness to pay

Used in an economic sense, demand has a very different significance, being equated with a person's willingness to pay for a specified good or service. Demand expressed in this way is often termed *effective demand*. Although the word 'pay' could refer to any financial or economic contribution, in practice it is usually equated with a cash payment.

This interpretation of demand implies that improved water supply and sanitation services are economic goods. Certainly, with some exceptions, governments in the developing world cannot afford to provide or sustain water and sanitation services without economic support. At the same time, there is strong evidence that many people are prepared to make significant economic contributions to receive services and service levels they desire.

By reflecting how people value an improved service, willingness to pay is a more reliable measure of demand than one based on an assumed level of affordability. Furthermore, various techniques have been developed to measure willingness to pay, associated with the presentation of a number of options. These facilitate its use as a practical design tool.

---

[1] See for example World Bank (1993). This shows that the proportion of income users spend on water varies considerably depending on local perceptions and circumstances. The research concludes that income is only one of many determinants of demand.

In spite of these arguments, there are legitimate concerns that such an approach may marginalise those least able to express their demands in the way or ways required - poor households and women in particular. Such groups are often unable to participate in decision making and influence the options on offer. At the same time, they may lack access to, or control over, the financial or economic resources used to measure their demand. It is these sections of society that remain largely unreached by most development projects.

2.3 Demand as an expression of a human right

Many of these issues are reflected in the rights based approach to development. The international human rights framework includes the right to a standard of living adequate for health and well-being[2], something that is implicit in the Millenium Development Goals[3]. This can only be achieved with access to safe water, adequate sanitation and an awareness of the associated health and hygiene issues.

It is debatable whether basic rights such as access to safe water and sanitation should be paid for by government (financed through some form of cross subsidy or taxation) or paid for by the individual concerned. Exceptionally, the Government of South Africa is now committed to provide free basic water[4] to all its citizens.

By way of contrast, the principles endorsed at the 1992 International Conference on Water and the Environment in Dublin require that *affordable* water and sanitation services be provided as a human right[5].

---

[2] The 1948 United Nations Universal Declaration of Human Rights refers to 'an adequate standard of living', although the term 'adequate' is undefined.

[3] Millenium Development Goals relating to water supply include halving the proportion of people who do not have access to affordable safe water by 2015.

[4] In South Africa, 'basic' refers to supplying each household with 6,000 litres of potable water per month from taps located within 200m of the dwelling. This is equivalent to 25 litres per capita day (pcd) for a family of eight. In practice, the extension of this policy to some rural areas is requiring a rethink of the 6,000 litre/200 metre standard, which is not always achievable.

[5] A summary of the Dublin Statement and its four guiding principles agreed at the International Conference on Water and the Environment in January 1992 can be found at http://www.dfid.gov.uk/.

The 4ᵗʰ Dublin principle

"Water has an economic value in all its competing uses and should be seen as an economic good. However, it is recognised that within this principle, it is vital to recognise the basic right of all human beings to have access to clean water and sanitation at an affordable price"

Since Dublin, the human rights agenda has advanced. Whilst access to basic services remains a fundamental concern, attention is now focused on how this can be achieved and in particular, how poor people can be engaged in development processes which affect their lives.

The human rights policy developed by the Department for International Development (DFID) is based on three cross-cutting principles:

Participation: enabling people to realise their rights to participate in, and access information relating to, the decision making processes that affect their lives.

Inclusion: building socially inclusive societies, based on the values of equality and non-discrimination, through development which promotes all human rights for all people.

Fulfilling obligation: strengthening institutions and policies which ensure that obligations to protect and promote the realisation of all human rights are fulfilled by states and other duty bearers.

DFID (2000)

In this context, it is important to note that human rights include the right to continuous improvements to living conditions and livelihood (Hausermann, 1999). Water and sanitation projects should be designed accordingly, underlining the importance of upgradable levels of service.

Whether associated with meeting basic needs or providing opportunities for self-development, the rights based view of demand emphasises the importance of ensuring that people are not treated as passive beneficiaries but are given a central role in decision making about the services and service levels they require.

2.4 Defining demand

Technical, economic and rights based views of demand are all valid in their specific context, but their use by different professionals involved in the same project can cause confusion. An unambiguous definition of demand is needed if the concept of designing to meet demand is to have any practical meaning. The definition used should satisfy a number of criteria:

- It should reflect how people value improved services rather than being based on external assumptions.

- It should stress the importance of users taking key decisions about the services and service levels they require.

- It should be applicable to vulnerable groups and individuals, above all, the poor and women who are often excluded from decision making.

- It should be practical, with expressions of demand being used as a tool to guide project design.

What is demand?

In these guidelines, 'demand' is defined *as an informed expression of desire for a particular service, assessed by the investments people are prepared to make, over the lifetime of the service, to receive and sustain it.*

The investments used to assess demand may consist of natural, economic, financial, human and social resources. Examples include the time and commitment used to plan, develop and sustain a water supply or sanitation project. Three additional points need emphasising:

- People must be informed of the characteristics of the services or facilities being offered and the implications of their choice. The latter includes all the inputs needed to receive and sustain a service.

- Meeting the demand of some users for higher levels of service may result in others being deprived. This could easily discriminate against those less able to articulate their demands unless specific precautions are taken.

- The poorest people in society have very limited access to the various resources that could be used to indicate demand. At the same time, what little they have may be fully committed as part of a day to day survival strategy. In such cases, it may be inappropriate for project staff to rely only on indicators of demand in the way described. A welfare approach may still be needed to ensure that the most vulnerable in a community are not excluded.

These points reinforce the fact that demand has important poverty and gender implications, factors which in practice are all too easily overlooked. Project staff must ensure that they are using indicators of demand that are appropriate for all the users concerned. Emphasis must be placed on establishing who is at risk of being marginalised. The poorest members of a community may need a locally appropriate, carefully targeted subsidy.

2.5 Stimulating demand

In Section, 1 it was pointed out that more people lack access to hygienic sanitation than remain without a safe, affordable water supply. Fundamentally, demand for sanitation may be weak because the perceived benefits of the improvements being offered do not compensate for the perceived costs.

The same may also apply if water quality is an issue. In some cases, people may prefer to use a contaminated water source for convenience, financial, cultural or aesthetic reasons. Demand for a safer water supply may need to be stimulated before users value it above a more risky alternative.

Stimulating demand involves developing and promoting options which embody the characteristics that people find most desirable, at a price they are willing to pay (a technique known as social marketing). Even so, a traditional practice or perception, may take years to change. More often than not, people's behaviour is modified over a period of time by their increasing exposure to the benefits of using an improved service. Further details of demand stimulation are provided in the following box.

Demand stimulation

In some cases, demand for sanitation or water supply may be weak or non-existent because the perceived benefits of whatever is being offered are out-weighed by the investments needed to receive and sustain it.

- In practice, perceptions may be poorly informed, or biased by the poor performance of past schemes or organisations.
- Alternatively, whatever is being offered is not based on people's perceptions of what is desirable.

In either case, demand for improved services may exist, but only in a hidden or *latent* form. The issue is how to unlock or stimulate latent demand.

Latent demand:

Demand that is not initially evident but revealed after people become aware of the potential benefits of an improved service. The improvements offered should reflect local (rather than external) perceptions of what is desirable and affordable.

Demand stimulation can be achieved by *social marketing*, a strategy that draws on conventional marketing techniques, albeit without an overriding profit motive. The strategy emphasises promoting the characteristics of a service that people find most attractive, at a price they are willing to pay. In the case of sanitation, these characteristics may include privacy, security, convenience, status and comfort, as well as potential health benefits. There is a risk that hygiene could become uncoupled from sanitation by pursuing such a strategy, and an appropriate hygiene promotion strategy would also be needed.

Demand stimulation involves changes in perception and behaviour, and this needs time to take hold. Once stimulated, demand can take off. For project managers, the challenge is how to devise a sustainable supply mechanism that can meet latent demand that is revealed in the future, long after project staff have left the scene.

3. Meeting demand

3.1 Factors which determine demand

Demand for water supply and sanitation is determined by a range of factors (see Figure 3.1), shaped by individual priorities and perceptions. Many individual demands are expressed at household level. Demand responsive projects should therefore focus on households. Inevitably, solutions may have to be negotiated at community or neighbourhood level, implying the need for collective decision making and skilled negotiation.

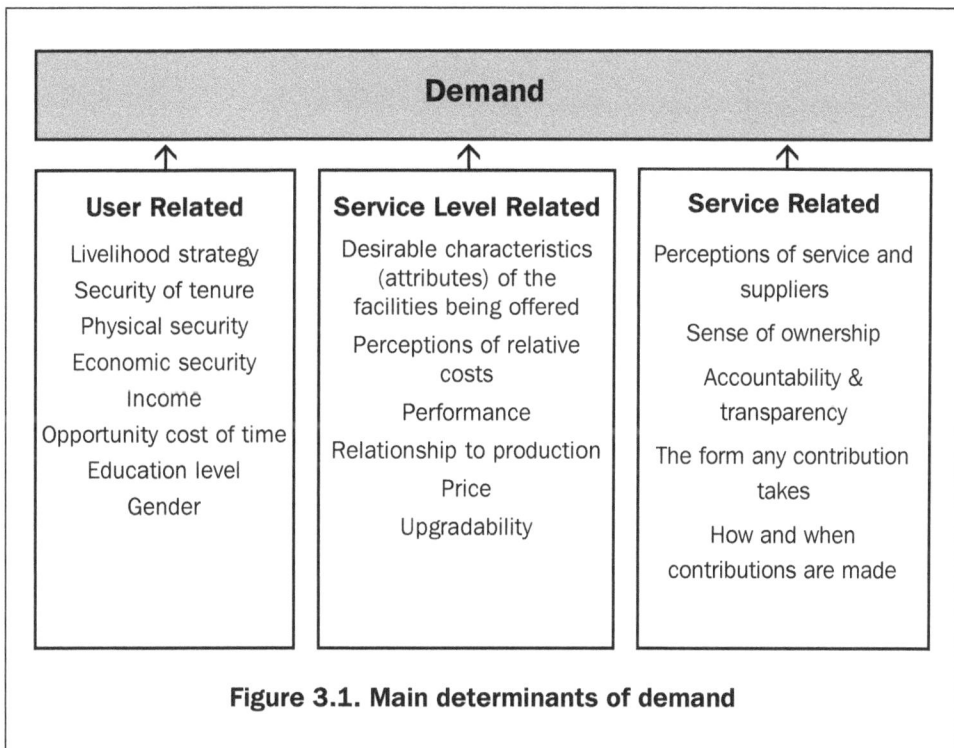

Demand		
User Related	**Service Level Related**	**Service Related**
Livelihood strategy	Desirable characteristics (attributes) of the facilities being offered	Perceptions of service and suppliers
Security of tenure		
Physical security		Sense of ownership
Economic security	Perceptions of relative costs	
Income		Accountability & transparency
Opportunity cost of time	Performance	
Education level	Relationship to production	The form any contribution takes
Gender	Price	
	Upgradability	How and when contributions are made

Figure 3.1. Main determinants of demand

Men tend to dominate household decision-making. Project staff have to ensure that the demands of women are not overlooked as a result. This may mean establishing alternative mechanisms for women to articulate their demand.

Of the factors identified in Figure 3.1, three in particular require further elaboration:

1. Service level and price
It is sometimes assumed that users will automatically want the cheapest level of service on offer. In fact, there is strong evidence that suggests that many people want - and are willing to pay for - higher levels of service.

For example, many people in peri-urban areas may opt to buy water from vendors rather than queue at a standpipe, possibly because this gives them time to engage in economic activities, or simply to reduce the drudgery and burden associated with fetching water. Similarly, in rural areas, some families living in homes made of traditional materials prefer to save up for a toilet with a cement block superstructure, rather than choosing a more affordable alternative.

2. Gender
The demands of men and women are rarely the same. Men and women often value the benefits of water and sanitation very differently, reflecting their specific roles and interests. In many cases, it is women who make the associated investment rather than men.

For example, in some cultures 'voluntary labour' and local materials are often supplied by women. Many women also pay for water with their own earnings, particularly if water is sold by the container at water points. Despite this, many studies have focused on investigating demand expressed by heads of households - usually adult males. Projects should reflect the demands of men *and* women, taking into account gender differences and the difficulties that women face in making their voices heard.

Parallel to the social and economic gender differences, the service levels offered should also reflect the different physical requirements of men, women and children. For further details see WEDC (forthcoming).

3. Relationship to production
Impact studies such as those undertaken by WaterAid (2001) have reinforced the important relationship between demand and the productive use of water. If water is provided in a form in which it can be used productively, for example,

to irrigate a kitchen garden, water livestock or manufacture building blocks, demand is likely to be higher.

The relationship between demand and production can be reinforced by the time savings associated with improved access to water. These provide the time to undertake such activities - as long as sufficient water is available. Clearly, environmental and other constraints must be taken into account, whilst project staff must ensure that women are not over-burdened as a result.

The importance of linking people, their economic activities and their environment is reflected in what is known as the sustainable livelihoods (SL) approach. This is summarised in the following box.

Demand and the sustainable livelihoods approach

A livelihood can be seen as the capacity, assets (a combination of social, human, financial, natural and physical resources) and activities needed to support a particular way of living.

The sustainable livelihoods (SL) approach uses this conceptual model as a framework to guide interventions. These are designed to have the greatest possible impact on poverty reduction, providing people with increased opportunities. Some measures focus on improving an asset base, reducing people's vulnerability to unexpected events, seasonal problems and longer term trends. The influence of other measures is less direct, focusing, for example, on policy change.

Using demand to guide project design can complement a SL approach, especially if policies support the provision of services for productive as well as health-related uses. For example, improved access to water can result in significant time-savings. The time saved, often by women, can be used productively - as can the water itself. Sanitation improvements, coupled with appropriate changes in hygiene behaviour, may reduce people's vulnerability to the impact of diarrhoeal disease.

Studies such as those conducted by WaterAid (2001) have also shown that time-savings and better sanitation result in stronger family bonds. In the livelihoods sense, strong social networks are also considered a resource. In summary, interventions are likely to support the livelihoods framework if they genuinely reflect people's demands.

3.2 Providing users with choice

Demand is met by enabling users to decide the type and form of service they are to receive. To achieve this, a number of potential options need to be identified and developed. These should reflect user perceptions and priorities, taking into account opportunities and constraints. This is shown schematically in Figure 3.2.

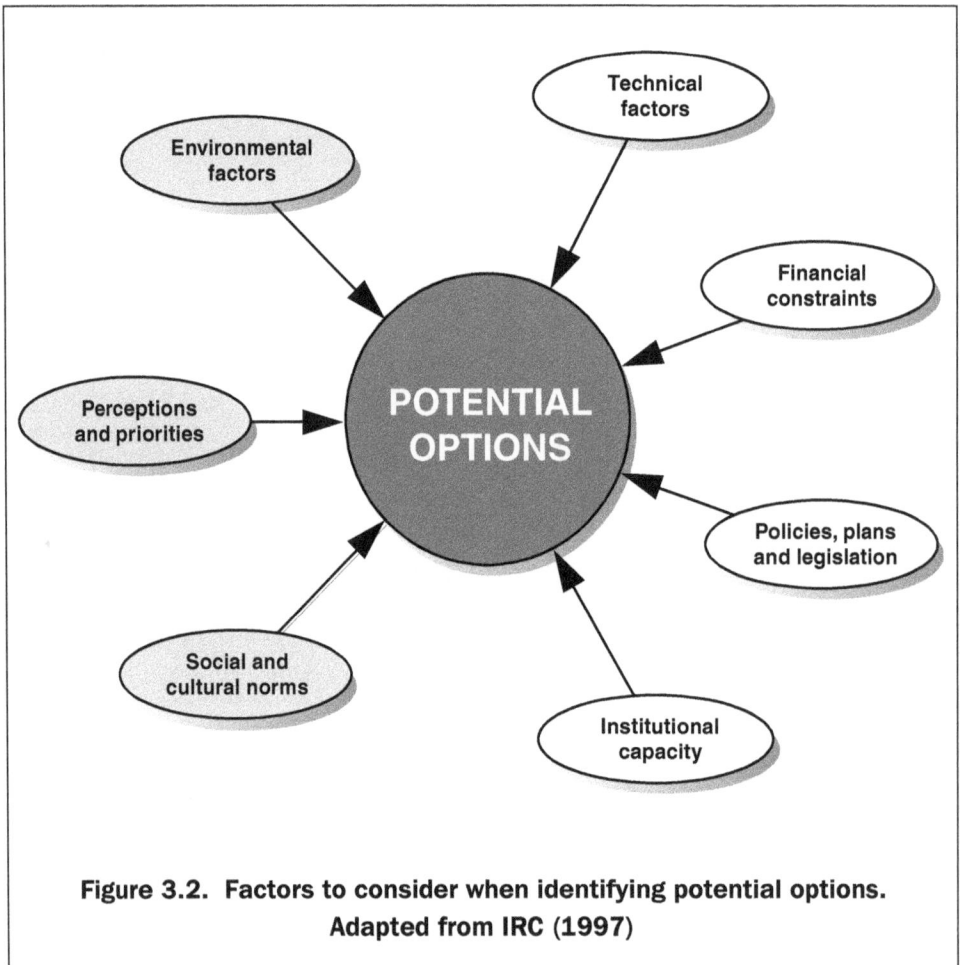

**Figure 3.2. Factors to consider when identifying potential options.
Adapted from IRC (1997)**

Relating demand to a service (rather than a level of service) has important consequences. Individually, users should be able to choose the level of service they desire and are prepared to sustain. Collectively, users should also be able to determine how resources are allocated, how a service is to be managed, and how contributions are to be made.

Once user preferences are known, these can be reflected in the project design. In practice it may be difficult or impossible to satisfy every choice, and a degree of consensus and compromise is inevitable.

3.3 The need for effective communication

Effective communication between users and project staff is vital if demand is to be met. For decision making to be meaningful, *all* users must be informed of the characteristics of each option and the broader implications of their choice. More generally, communities need to know how to contact organisations responsible for implementing projects. This can be a particular problem in remote rural areas.

For their part, project staff must be able to identify and measure appropriate expressions of demand. The final design may have to be negotiated, balancing user demands with what is technically feasible, environmentally sustainable, institutionally supportable and economically justified.

Perceptions of being able to communicate easily with households, individually and collectively, may be optimistic. Many people find it difficult to participate: the poor often have to work long hours away from home, whilst women can be culturally inhibited from attending meetings or expressing their views. The poor are also the least likely to have the confidence to come forward and articulate their demand.

Skilled facilitation is therefore required (as well as additional time) to seek out the disadvantaged and ensure their inclusion. Engineers must be willing and able to become involved in a constructive dialogue with users. This involves an exchange of technical ideas and concepts, adopting an advisory rather than an instructive role. For this reason, most engineers would benefit from training in the use of participatory techniques. Equally, social facilitators may need a basic understanding of technical issues.

4. Demand assessment

Having defined demand and considered how it can be met through the identification and development of an appropriate selection of options, it is important to consider how demand can be assessed. A number of techniques can be used:

- Investigating people's coping strategies.

- Demonstrations of demand.

- User participation in option development.

- Contingent valuation (this may only be useful for larger projects in peri-urban areas).

Whichever method is used, demand is difficult to assess and may change over the course of a project. It is therefore good practice to use a number of techniques to confirm demand.

4.1 Investigating coping strategies

Demand can be predicted by investigating people's coping strategies related to water supply and sanitation. These have been developed by communities, households and individuals to sustain or improve a livelihood. The information obtained, supported by data from primary and secondary sources, can be used to develop a demand responsive project strategy.

Such an investigation can take the form of a detailed socio-economic survey, in which case it is known as a revealed preference study. Coping strategies can also be assessed rather less formally, using a number of participatory techniques as well as field observations to obtain an overview of likely demand across a wide area.

In either case, the following information could help predict future demand for improved services:

- The amount of time spent fetching water; the volume used, its quality, and where and how it is used.

- The type and size of any associated investment, who is making it and how it is made.

- Evidence of community meetings to consider how to sustain or improve an existing water supply.

- Efforts made, individually or collectively, to maintain or upgrade an existing water supply (this includes unauthorised connections and investments in water storage.

- Efforts made to dispose of (or otherwise manage) excreta. This may be demonstrated by one or two households rather than by the community as a whole. Such 'positive deviance' provides project staff with clues as to what may be successful.

- Efforts made to improve the household and public environment, for example, by keeping the area around the home clear of rubbish.

- Expenditure on health, related to the treatment of illnesses associated with inadequate sanitation.

For further details on the use of coping studies to assess demand, see Section 8.2.1 in Part II of this booklet.

4.2 Demonstrations of demand

The contributions people make in return for receiving a service provide project staff with a useful series of demand-based indicators that can be used to keep a demand responsive project on track. Some examples, used by our research collaborators, are shown in Table 4.1.

Linking contributions with demand

Contributions of cash, time and materials can only be considered as demonstrations of demand if they are clearly linked with the service and service levels being provided. People have to understand why contributions are needed and how they will be used.

Demonstrations of demand can be used by project staff to indicate how effective the service options being offered will be in terms of meeting community, household and individual demands. In this respect, it is important to identify those groups and individuals who are *not* demonstrating their demand, and investigate why this is the case.

Table 4.1. Demonstrations of demand used during the project process	
Stage in project process	**Demonstration of demand**
Project selection	Application form completed and signed
	Community meetings held
	Village clean up campaign
Planning	Water and/or sanitation committee appointed
	Bank account opened
	Focus groups formed and sustained
	Participation in baseline data collection
	Community action plan prepared
	Cash or other contributions made[6]
Appraisal	Demand tested by users selecting their preferred options, knowing the implications of their choice.
	Contract signed between community, implementing organisation and local government
Implementation	Contributions of cash, materials, time and labour linked to specific services and service levels
Operation	Maintenance contributions collected
	Upgrading and extending levels of service

---

[6] At this stage of the project, a cash contribution can also be used to indicate a community's ability to organise and collect payments.

Reflecting the importance of linking contributions with the delivery of services, the quality of the indicators used to demonstrate demand has to be monitored. For example, in the case of a cash contribution, some households may be forced into making payments by a powerful elite. Alternatively, an unscrupulous contractor could provide all the funds required in return for the promise of a lucrative contract.

4.3 User participation in option development

One of the most effective ways to ensure that demand is met is to involve users in option identification and development. In effect, demand is being continuously assessed and responded to as an integral part of the design process.

In order to achieve this in practice, appropriate mechanisms are required that enable users to participate. For example, representatives of different focus groups could be appointed to act as a 'design board'. This is quite different from the idea of a local committee taking managerial decisions; community management may be one of several management options. For further information about user participation in option development, including a number of practical tools and examples, see Section 10.3.

4.4 Contingent valuation

The last way of assessing demand to be considered is known as contingent valuation. This involves a range of options being described to users, either individually in the form of a one-to-one interview, or collectively as part of a focus group discussion. Users are then asked to state what they would be willing to pay in order to receive a particular service. To facilitate this process, those participating may be presented with a range of prices in the form of a bidding game[7].

---

[7] A bidding game is designed to establish the maximum an individual is prepared to pay for a specified service. A number of prices are suggested in turn and the respondent asked whether or not he or she would be prepared to pay these until the limit is found. This is not as simple as it sounds. There are many factors which may lead people to give misleading results. For further details see Wedgwood & Sansom (2001).

The prices suggested must reflect the costs of supplying or sustaining an option. Estimating this can be quite difficult especially if the cost of an option depends in part on its popularity.

Contingent valuation[8] is often associated with a comprehensive household survey and individual interviews. The results are then processed using statistical methods to identify and rule out bias. Not surprisingly, this process is expensive and its use in peri-urban and rural areas is somewhat limited.

Recently a number of techniques have been developed combining elements of contingent valuation and participatory development. These are less robust statistically but more practical and affordable to implement. An example is described later on in Section 10.4.2.

---

[8] Contingent valuation is described as such because people are asked to value a number of options that do not at the time exist. Their response depends on (or is contingent on) these options being delivered as they are described.

5. Additional factors to consider

As previously emphasised, using demand as a tool to design projects has limitations, many of which concern the potential marginalisation of those less able to express their demands. A number of other considerations should also be taken into account, some of which are listed below.

■ Demand can be influenced by politicians, for example, by promising free water. Willingness to pay is sometimes negated by a politically based unwillingness to charge.

■ The local policy, institutional and legal environment may reflect supply driven rather than demand driven priorities.

■ People may have unrealistic expectations of the level of service they can afford, or may feel that they are entitled to a free service.

■ The impact of past experience (for example, concerning the use of one technology) may skew demand in a particular direction.

■ Technologies are often associated with economies of scale. Offering a mix of technologies to satisfy demand for different service levels can result in the least popular becoming unaffordable.

■ Water may be required for a variety of purposes. Many water supply projects focus on its provision for domestic use only.

■ Users may not put much weight on the potential health risks of consuming unsafe water when selecting an option.

■ Very poor people will continue to need subsidies. Subsidies will have to be carefully targeted in order that they complement, rather than distort, demand.

■ Participatory approaches and collective decision making may be dominated by an elite, in order to favour their interests.

■ Demand can change considerably as the population changes and circumstances and perceptions are altered.

■ Options can be very limited, for example in a water-scarce rural area. In such cases, decision making about service levels may be limited to siting a single well or handpump.

Together, these points make the process of meeting demand complicated and can add significantly to the time and resources needed to plan and implement a project.

Ultimately donors, policy makers and project staff must decide the extent to which they can be demand responsive, balancing improved impact and sustainability with the limited capacity, resources and time available. Introducing the demand concept incrementally, and learning from and refining the approach used, is probably the most effective way forward for many implementing organisations. For further details, see Book 2 of these guidelines, Additional Notes for Policy Makers and Planners.

6. Principles of meeting demand

The points discussed in the previous sections are reflected in a set of eight principles. These should help project staff design practical, locally appropriate strategies that are also poverty and gender sensitive.

Principles of meeting demand

1. An effective project communication strategy is devised which enables project staff to engage with communities, households and individuals.

2. Systems for individual and collective decision-making are established and used.

3. Appropriate indicators of demand are identified and used to assess demand.

4. Options are identified, developed and priced which:
   - Are based on user priorities and perceptions of value.
   - Are socially and culturally acceptable.
   - Reflect supply costs.
   - Reflect local and regional development policies and plans.
   - Are environmentally, technically and financially feasible.

5. People are enabled to make an informed choice of:
   - How they can participate in a project.
   - Service level options.
   - How services are to be allocated, managed and maintained.
   - How contributions are to be made and managed.

6. Specific provision is made to ensure that all groups and individuals within a community can participate in the process. This ensures that vulnerable people such as women and the poor are included and that their demands are reflected in the services provided.

7. If necessary, demand should be stimulated by promoting the potential benefits of the options being offered, ensuring that these options reflect user perceptions.

8. Facilities are designed and management systems are established which are capable of responding to future changes in demand.

What next?

Part II of these guidelines introduces a typical project cycle. This is 'unwound' in order to form the step-by-step process of development experienced by users rather than project staff or donors. At each stage it is demonstrated how demand can be used as a practical design tool to improve the impact and sustainability of the services provided.

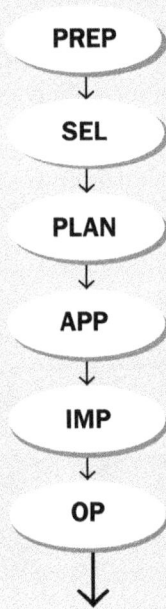

Flow		Key
PREP ↓		
SEL ↓	**Prep**:	Preparing a project strategy
PLAN ↓	**Sel**:	Selecting a community sub-project
APP ↓	**Plan**:	Developing a community plan
IMP ↓	**App**:	Appraisal
OP ↓	**Imp**:	Implementation
	Op:	Operation, maintenance & management

Within this framework, it is shown how appropriate options which are capable of meeting demand can be identified, developed, priced, tested and offered.

The limitations of using demand to guide project design are highlighted in order that the concept can be used effectively. Various techniques that can improve the participation of vulnerable communities, groups and individuals in decision making are described. There is however no demand-responsive blueprint. It is up to those implementing projects to develop an appropriate response, taking into account the local context and their own capacity.

Designing water supply and sanitation projects
to meet demand in rural and peri-urban communities

Part II:
Practice

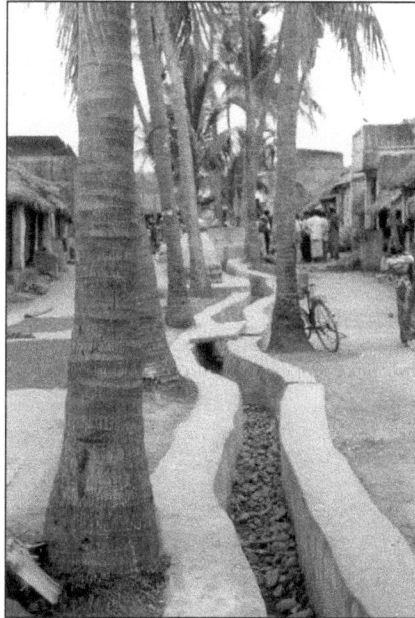

Street drainage in a village in Ganjam District, Orissa.
Villagers decided to route the channel between the trees rather than cut them down.

Practice: Summary

In Part II, the conventional project cycle is 'unwound' to produce the sequence of events that those living in a community experience. At each stage, it is demonstrated how expressions of demand can be used as a tool to guide the project towards a more sustainable outcome and services which are used.

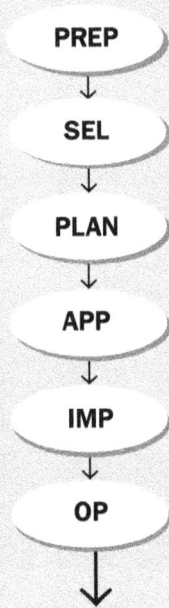

Flowchart	Key
PREP	**Key**
↓	
SEL	**Prep:** Preparing a project strategy
↓	
PLAN	**Sel:** Selecting a community sub-project
↓	
APP	**Plan:** Developing a community plan
↓	
IMP	**App:** Appraisal
↓	
OP	**Imp:** Implementation
↓	**Op:** Operation, maintenance and management

Designing for demand therefore concerns the entire project process. It is not just about the design and delivery of infrastructure. What happens after implementation is critically important for sustainability. Management systems, cost recovery, maintenance and how to upgrade and extend services must be addressed and as such are fundamental components of the project's overall design.

In Part I of this booklet, demand has been defined as: *an informed expression of desire for a particular service, measured by the investments people are prepared to make to receive and sustain it*. Now Part II demonstrates how project staff can work with demand to:

■ Guide the development of a project strategy.
■ Help identify which individuals, households and communities are at risk of exclusion.
■ Help prioritise communities for development activity.
■ Appraise a community plan.
■ Develop a range of options.
■ Help a local management organisation to sustain the facilities provided.

In particular, Part II describes how project staff can identify, develop, cost, price and offer appropriate options which are capable of meeting the demands of all users.

The engineer's role

The final section of these guidelines considers the implications of designing to meet demand, focusing on project engineers. Engineers have traditionally derived much of their authority from the technical decisions they make and the importance of infrastructure. A demand responsive approach can challenge this state of affairs. This last section clarifies the engineer's role, and shows how, for engineers willing to engage with the people they serve, the process can be stimulating, challenging and highly rewarding.

Principles of meeting demand

1. An effective project communication strategy is devised which enables project staff to engage with communities, households and individuals.

2. Systems for individual and collective decision-making are established and used.

3. Appropriate indicators of demand are identified and used to assess demand.

4. Options are identified, developed and priced which:
   - Are based on user priorities and perceptions of value.
   - Are socially and culturally acceptable.
   - Reflect supply costs.
   - Reflect local and regional development policies and plans.
   - Are environmentally, technically and financially feasible.

5. People are enabled to make an informed choice of:
   - How they can participate in a project.
   - Service level options.
   - How services are to be allocated, managed and maintained.
   - How contributions are to be made and managed.

6. Specific provision is made to ensure that all groups and individuals within a community can participate in the process. This ensures that vulnerable people such as women and the poor are included and that their demands are reflected in the services provided.

7. If necessary, demand should be stimulated by promoting the potential benefits of the options being offered, ensuring that these options reflect user perceptions.

8. Facilities are designed and management systems are established which are capable of responding to future changes in demand.

7. The project process

For planners, funders and project managers, the project cycle provides a useful basis on which to design and implement strategies and programmes (see Figure 7.1). The continuous sequence reflects an external point of view that would not be recognisable to the users themselves.

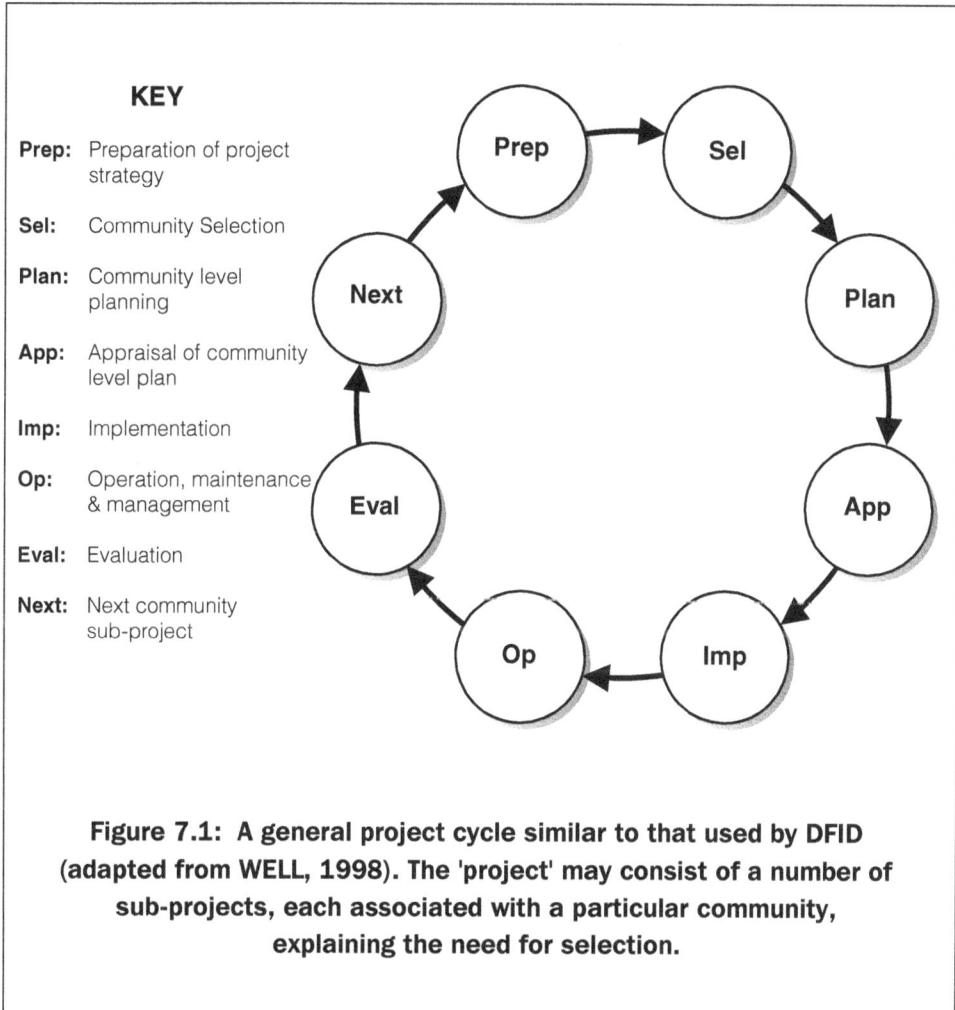

KEY

Prep: Preparation of project strategy

Sel: Community Selection

Plan: Community level planning

App: Appraisal of community level plan

Imp: Implementation

Op: Operation, maintenance & management

Eval: Evaluation

Next: Next community sub-project

Figure 7.1: A general project cycle similar to that used by DFID (adapted from WELL, 1998). The 'project' may consist of a number of sub-projects, each associated with a particular community, explaining the need for selection.

The terminology used to describe each stage in the project cycle varies from organisation to organisation. In these guidelines, the term 'preparation' refers to activities associated with the development of a project strategy. Selection is only relevant if one has to prioritise on a number of sub-projects.

The emphasis of many externally funded projects tends to encourage implementing organisations to view service delivery in terms of the time-bound supply of infrastructure or other investments. As a result, most emphasis is put on implementation and the construction of infrastructure.

The aim of using a demand based approach is to improve the impact and sustainability of the services provided. This implies that the focus should shift from the donor agency to the users' perspective, and from implementation to operation[9]. With this in mind, it is useful to 'unwind' the project cycle, in order to see things from a user perspective.

Designing to meet demand influences what is undertaken at each stage of the resulting linear process. This is summarised in Figure 7.2.

7.1 The special case of sanitation

The characteristics of sanitation - in particular, domestic sanitation, and water supply are very different. For example:

■ Sanitation is usually a household issue affecting families and individuals rather than communities. In this respect it is a private good. This is reflected in the allocation of responsibilities in terms of acquiring and maintaining facilities.

■ Sanitation practices and related behaviours are often long established, reflecting cultural and social values to a greater extent than water supply.

---

[9] In the case of sanitation, 'operation' would include the scaling up of service delivery in response to increasing demand, after project staff have left the area.

■ Demand for improved sanitation facilities is often weak or non-existent and must be stimulated before it can be responded to. This cannot be a one-off activity. It requires exposure, understanding and behavioural change over a period of time which often exceeds the project's timeframe.

As a result, sanitation requires a sustainable *supply* mechanism that can continue to stimulate demand, facilitate the acquisition of latrines by households and promote appropriate *hygiene behaviours after the project team has left the scene*. This is reflected in Figure 7.3, which shows the project process from a sanitation perspective.

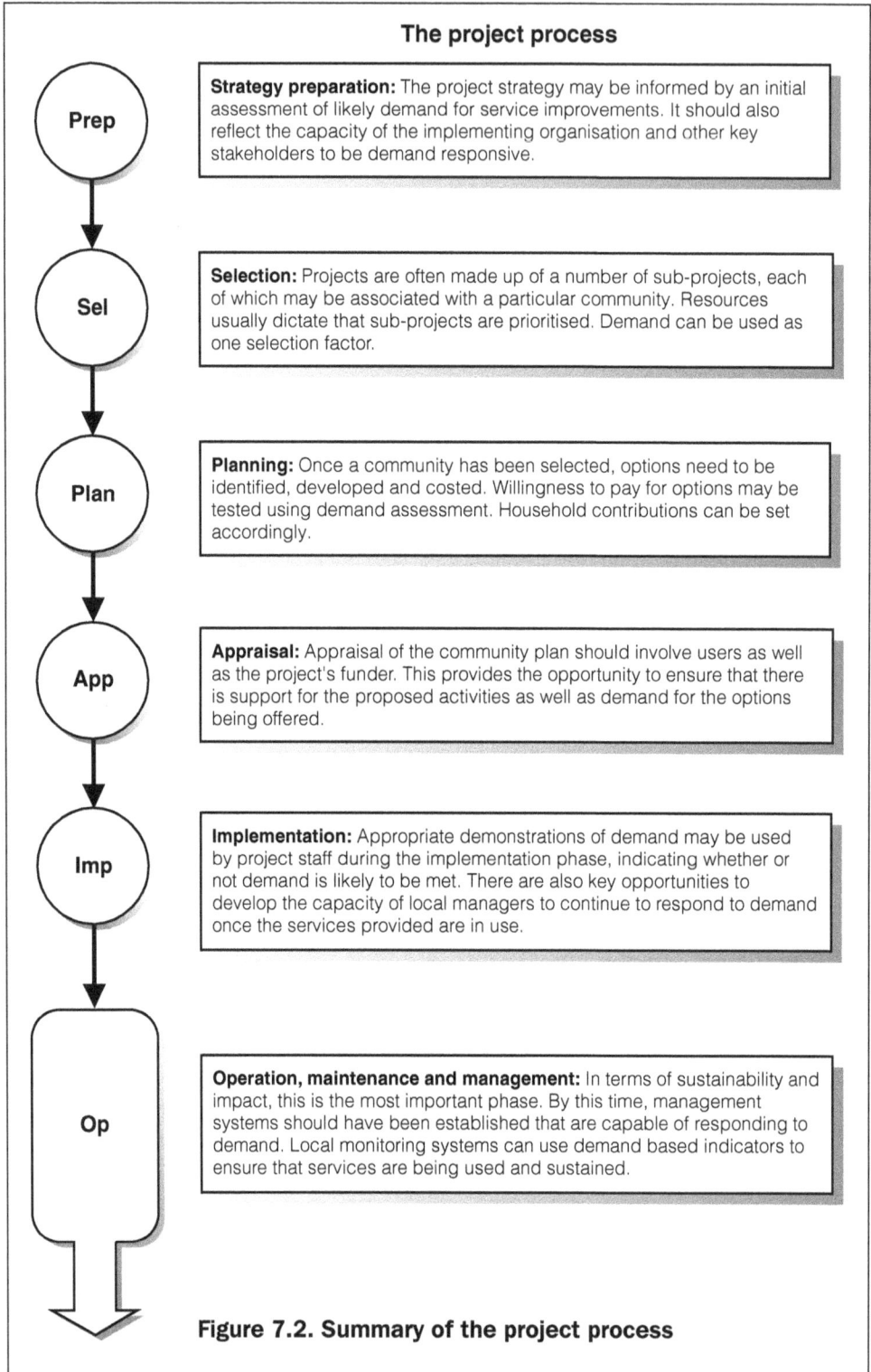

The project process

Prep

Strategy preparation: The project strategy may be informed by an initial assessment of likely demand for service improvements. It should also reflect the capacity of the implementing organisation and other key stakeholders to be demand responsive.

Sel

Selection: Projects are often made up of a number of sub-projects, each of which may be associated with a particular community. Resources usually dictate that sub-projects are prioritised. Demand can be used as one selection factor.

Plan

Planning: Once a community has been selected, options need to be identified, developed and costed. Willingness to pay for options may be tested using demand assessment. Household contributions can be set accordingly.

App

Appraisal: Appraisal of the community plan should involve users as well as the project's funder. This provides the opportunity to ensure that there is support for the proposed activities as well as demand for the options being offered.

Imp

Implementation: Appropriate demonstrations of demand may be used by project staff during the implementation phase, indicating whether or not demand is likely to be met. There are also key opportunities to develop the capacity of local managers to continue to respond to demand once the services provided are in use.

Op

Operation, maintenance and management: In terms of sustainability and impact, this is the most important phase. By this time, management systems should have been established that are capable of responding to demand. Local monitoring systems can use demand based indicators to ensure that services are being used and sustained.

Figure 7.2. Summary of the project process

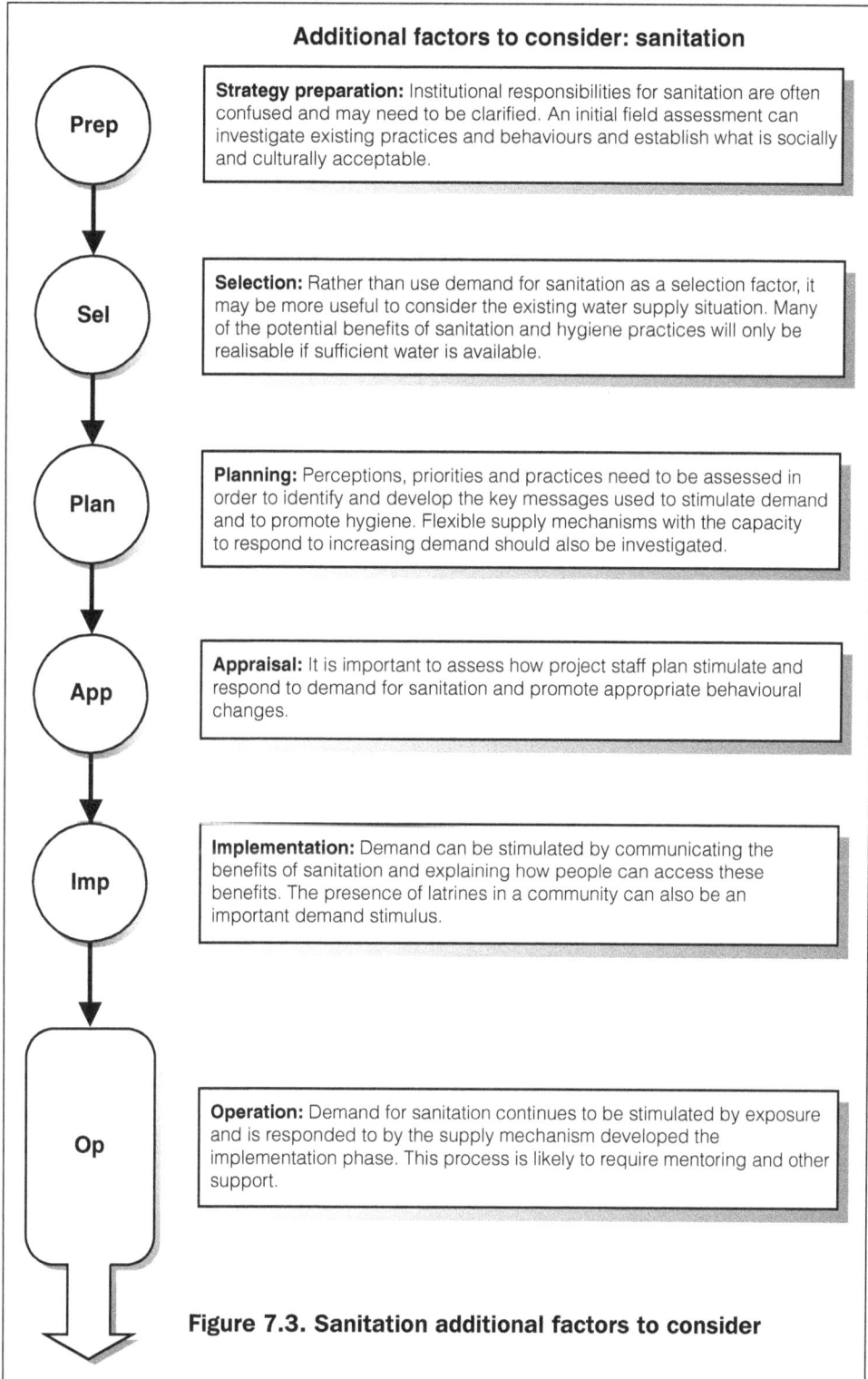

Additional factors to consider: sanitation

Prep

Strategy preparation: Institutional responsibilities for sanitation are often confused and may need to be clarified. An initial field assessment can investigate existing practices and behaviours and establish what is socially and culturally acceptable.

Sel

Selection: Rather than use demand for sanitation as a selection factor, it may be more useful to consider the existing water supply situation. Many of the potential benefits of sanitation and hygiene practices will only be realisable if sufficient water is available.

Plan

Planning: Perceptions, priorities and practices need to be assessed in order to identify and develop the key messages used to stimulate demand and to promote hygiene. Flexible supply mechanisms with the capacity to respond to increasing demand should also be investigated.

App

Appraisal: It is important to assess how project staff plan stimulate and respond to demand for sanitation and promote appropriate behavioural changes.

Imp

Implementation: Demand can be stimulated by communicating the benefits of sanitation and explaining how people can access these benefits. The presence of latrines in a community can also be an important demand stimulus.

Op

Operation: Demand for sanitation continues to be stimulated by exposure and is responded to by the supply mechanism developed the implementation phase. This process is likely to require mentoring and other support.

Figure 7.3. Sanitation additional factors to consider

7.2 Packaging water supply, sanitation and hygiene

Integrating water supply, sanitation and hygiene promotion into a single 'package' is often justified on impact and efficiency grounds. However, there is strong evidence that when this is done, sanitation and hygiene are often neglected in favour of water supply. Similarly, hygiene is often neglected in stand-alone sanitation projects (Leblanc, 2001).

There is no single reason why this is the case. Certainly, the skills required for sanitation and hygiene differ significantly from those needed by water supply, and may not be available. This reflects that whilst water supply is often perceived by users as a community issue, sanitation and hygiene are perceived as individual or household concerns. Furthermore, demand for sanitation is often weak and needs to be stimulated. As a result, the skills required by practitioners are social rather than technical.

The issue of demand introduces further challenges to implementing a package approach. This is because the project team is expected to carry out three very different tasks in a limited time frame:

■ Respond to existing demand (usually associated with water supply).

■ Identify and promote appropriate hygiene behaviour change.

■ Stimulate demand (in particular, for sanitation).

Evidence from South East Asia suggests that a sanitation programme may take eight or more years to implement (Mukherjee, 2001). This reflects the time required by people to change or adapt long established practices and perceptions. Many families only decide to improve their sanitation facilities after they have seen the benefits being realised by a neighbour or relation who has one. Inevitably, take up can be slow.

There is a clear risk that project staff and users themselves focus on responding to demand for improved water supplies. Time and resources (both human and financial) have to be reserved for each of the three activities listed above. Alternatively, water, sanitation and hygiene interventions can be co-ordinated but implemented as separate, co-ordinated projects.

```
(PREP) ──▶ (SEL) ──▶ (PLAN) ──▶ (APP) ──▶ (IMP) ──▶ (OP) ⟹
```

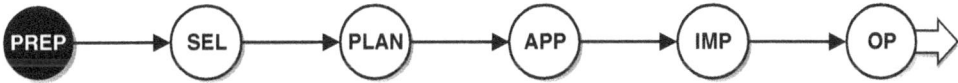

8. Preparing a project strategy

In many respects, the first step in the project process is one of the most important as it is then that key relationships are forged, responsibilities agreed and a project's aims, objectives and strategy defined. These may be difficult to change at a later stage. At this stage, project staff undertake a number of activities. These are likely to include:

- Agreeing overall project objectives, major activities and outputs.

- Defining overall geographical boundaries for the project area.

- Establishing key institutional linkages, roles and responsibilities.

- Designing activities for each objective, estimating the resources required.

- Establishing the basis for a project management system.

- Identifying and training project staff.

- Agreeing, and if necessary testing the methodologies to be used with project partners and stakeholders.

Adapted from Ockelford and Reed (2000).

Such activities should lead to the development of an effective project strategy. However, in order to be effective, this strategy should also reflect demand for improved services, as well as any major constraints that may limit the ability of project staff to respond in return.

In this respect, three important measures can be used that can help project staff develop an effective demand-based strategy and build their own capacity (and that of their partners) to respond at the same time. These are:

1. A detailed investigation of the project's policy, legislative and institutional environment, specifically focusing on the opportunities and constraints related to the demands of users.

2. An initial assessment of demand for service improvements. This may involve an investigation of people's coping strategies or, in some cases, the use of contingent valuation.

3. A review of potential technical, management and contribution related options that may be applicable to the local situation.

Whatever is planned at this stage should take into account the risk of not being able to proceed with a project or sub-project. In particular, the impact of raising unrealisable expectations can be very detrimental to a community. Care has also to be taken to balance the quality of the information needed with the resources required and the risk that the resulting strategy may not be approved. An overview is needed rather than detail.

Overview rather than detail

If a project consists of a number of sub-projects (often each of these is associated with a community), it is important to get an overview rather than detailed information. This is because the detailed findings from one location may not be transferable to another. Assessing demand using a relatively expensive and location-specific contingent valuation technique (see Section 8.2.2) should only be undertaken when project staff are confident that work is going to start in the community involved.

Undertaking the measures mentioned exposes project staff and partners to the concept of demand, strengthening their capacity to be responsive later on in the project process. Each measure will now be looked at in more detail.

8.1 Investigating the enabling environment

A project strategy should reflect its 'external' environment, which is made up of policies, legislation and institutions. Together these can have a profound influence (both in terms of opportunities and constraints) on the extent that expressions of demand can be used to guide project design.

Whilst some investigations may involve a review of existing data, it is also important to establish a constructive dialogue with the key stakeholders involved. This provides the opportunity to introduce the project, clarify its aims and objectives, develop a working relationship and discuss points of concern in more detail.

Table 8.1 identifies some of the key issues that could be investigated. The table is not exhaustive and may include issues that are not always relevant.

Table 8.1. Factors to consider when investigating the enabling environment

Issue	Possible points to be investigated
Policy	■ What are the local, regional and national priorities and plans related to service provision and water resource management? Does the proposed project comply?
	■ Do selection criteria exist to prioritise communities or households for water supply and sanitation improvements? Who selects sub-projects?
	■ For what purposes may water be provided?
	■ What is understood by sanitation? Does the word include broader aspects of environmental sanitation, such as refuse disposal and drainage?
	■ Are basic service levels for water and sanitation defined? If so, how? Are certain types of technology favoured or proscribed?
	■ Are institutional responsibilities for service provision and support defined? For example, what role could the local private sector play in the longer-term delivery of sanitation?
	■ Are contribution levels (towards capital, recurrent and replacement costs) defined? If so, how?
	■ What is the current policy on subsidies? Are rules rigid, or is there scope for flexibility and targeting?
	■ What is the policy on cost limits? How much scope for flexibility is there?
	■ Are funds available to start up savings and credit schemes designed to make services more affordable?
	■ What are the technical specifications, norms or standards, applying to: - Infrastructure design and levels of service? - Water quality and quantity? - Ground-water contamination?
Legislation	■ Is the local management organisation authorised to propose, implement and operate projects, form contracts, make by-laws, set tariffs and collect payments?
	■ How effective is the water or sanitation committee registration process?
	■ Is local government mandated to support service provision?
Institutional	■ What is the actual capacity of local government, the private sector and non-governmental organisations to plan, implement and sustain projects?

8.2 Assessing likely demand

Assessing likely demand for improved water supply and sanitation services is an important part of formulating a demand responsive project strategy. Depending on the circumstances, two techniques could be used: an investigation of people's coping strategies and contingent valuation.

8.2.1 Investigating coping strategies

Many water supply and sanitation projects encompass large, diverse populations, living in a number of communities. These could be rural settlements or in the case of a peri-urban area, individual streets or wards. At this stage, project staff are unlikely to know exactly where they are going to start work, or even how communities are going to be prioritised.

In these circumstances what is needed is an overview. This should capture the social, cultural, economic and physical conditions present throughout the project area, identifying the coping strategies, knowledge and skills of the population.

What is a coping strategy?

A behaviour or practice employed by people to maintain or improve an existing lifestyle or livelihood. A study of coping strategies can reveal useful information about people's perceptions, priorities and demand for improved services, without building excessive expectations.

The information required can be obtained by direct observation or a detailed survey. The latter is sometimes called a *revealed preference survey* and is an established socio-economic technique. The design, piloting and analysis of a survey is however relatively complex, requiring specialist advice. Neither are the detailed results obtained transferable from one community to another.

Like contingent valuation, it is probably only worthwhile in densely populated areas and where project staff are confident that the results will be used[10]. By comparison, field observations of coping strategies can cover more ground, raise fewer expectations and still produce good results, especially if supported by a number of small group discussions and semi-structured interviews. Secondary data could be used to plan the field assessment. Care has to be taken to include a cross section of communities, households or individuals, ensuring that vulnerable groups have not been excluded. The following type of information could be collected.

Water supply

- The amount of time and effort spent fetching water; the quantity used, the quality preferred and why; and what water is used for.

- Efforts made at household or community level to maintain or improve existing services, including evidence of economic investments being made, upgrading (see below) and organisation (for example, meetings held to consider possible improvements).

- The presence of unauthorised connections to an existing piped water supply.

- Evidence of a local welfare system or safety net that helps ensure a degree of equity in terms of access to water.

Sanitation

- Efforts made to improve existing sanitation practices, for example, digging pits, keeping latrines clean, digging new pits when required and disposing of children's faeces.

- Efforts made to improve environmental sanitation in its wider sense, for example, keeping the area around the home clear of domestic animals and rubbish.

- Efforts made to improve health, especially that of infants and children. This is also related to hygiene promotion.

---

[10] For further information about planning and conducting a revealed preference survey, and the use of surveys in general, see MacGranahan et al (1997).

- The resources, including financial resources, used to treat illness associated with poor sanitation.

General

- Economic status of households as communities, possibly based on locally developed indicators and participatory assessment.

- Details of indigenous decision-making or contribution systems. This may not be directly related to water supply or sanitation.

- The existence of traditional networks - often a starting point for understanding exclusion and ensuring inclusion.

- Details of relevant skills and expertise available in the area. Indigenous skills (and the use of local materials or construction techniques) are often overlooked by project staff.

- The existence and capacity of the small-scale private sector to play a role in service delivery.

Measuring ability to pay

Some projects attempt to estimate demand by measuring people's ability to pay. Rather than establish household income, this may be done by using a number of substitute or proxy indicators which are easier to assess. For example, physical assets such as a tin roof or a television set may imply a certain standard of living. This is then associated with demand for a particular service level.

In practice it is difficult to assess demand in this way because it makes critical assumptions about how people value improved services.

Nevertheless, developing an understanding of people's economic status is important for the design of poverty-sensitive strategies. One example illustrating how this can be done is described in Box 10.9. in Section 10.4.4.

In terms of developing an effective project strategy, the results from an investigation of coping strategies could be used in a number of ways:

- To establish the general characteristics of services (and service levels) that people seem to prefer and why. This may have important implications for staff training and selection.

- To identify a lack of demand, explore why it is weak, and establish the focus of measures designed to stimulate demand.

- To establish the type of contribution that people may be willing and able to make and identify opportunities for cross subsidy.

- To identify the degree and nature of social differentiation that occurs across the project area.

- To identify possible management, contribution and service delivery options.

- To identify appropriate communication channels and media that can be used to initiate a dialogue with potential users.

8.2.2 Contingent valuation

Another technique which could be used to assess likely demand is known as contingent valuation, in which potential options are described to a sample of users. People are then asked to say how much they would be willing to pay[11], selecting their response from a range of prices. The process takes the form of a structured interview between a householder and a trained enumerator.

What is contingent valuation?

A demand assessment technique based on describing a number of service options to potential users and asking how much they would be willing to pay to receive or sustain them.

---

[11] In this context, the word pay does not necessarily mean 'with cash' but may refer to any economic contribution.

At this stage in the project process, contingent valuation has limited application. The technique normally requires a degree of expertise above that required by a revealed preference survey (see Section 8.2.1). This makes it relatively expensive. At the same time, the detailed results obtained may not be transferable to other communities. Finally, contingent valuation can only be used if:

■ Project staff have established a range of feasible options which are likely to capture demand.

■ Project staff can provide users with a good estimate of how much these options will cost.

In some cases, this information may be available - for example, this may be the case in a town where the existing piped water supply is to be extended into a previously 'unserved' ward[12]. In most peri-urban and rural areas, however, demand assessment based on a more general study of people's copying strategies will be the better choice. Contingent valuation can also be used to confirm demand for fully developed options later on in a project. This is described in Section 10.4.2.

8.3 Seasonality

People's priorities, preferences and their demand often depends on the season or time of year, especially in rural areas. A useful tool that can be used to investigate this relationship is called the social calendar. This is based on the participatory development of a graphical chart or timeline in which activities are described for each season. One example, extracted from GTZ's handbook on gender sensitive participatory approaches (GTZ, 1995) is shown in Figure 8.1. This shows the different tasks undertaken by men and women.

Seasonal and gender sensitive information of this sort can be used to plan how to implement a project. This has been done by the Rural Water Supply and Sanitation Fund Development Board in Nepal: its three-year implementation cycle is designed to fit the availability of resources in the Himalayan foothills. Communities are encouraged to adapt the implementation framework pro-

---

[12] For an example demonstrating the use of contingent valuation in Lugazi, Uganda, see the report by Whittington et al (1998).

vided to suit their unique circumstances. This is particularly important for latrine construction which is often confined to a particular season. This is reflected in Figure 8.1, which suggests that men and women may have more time to undertake such tasks between planting and harvesting their crops. This should be continued by follow up discussions.

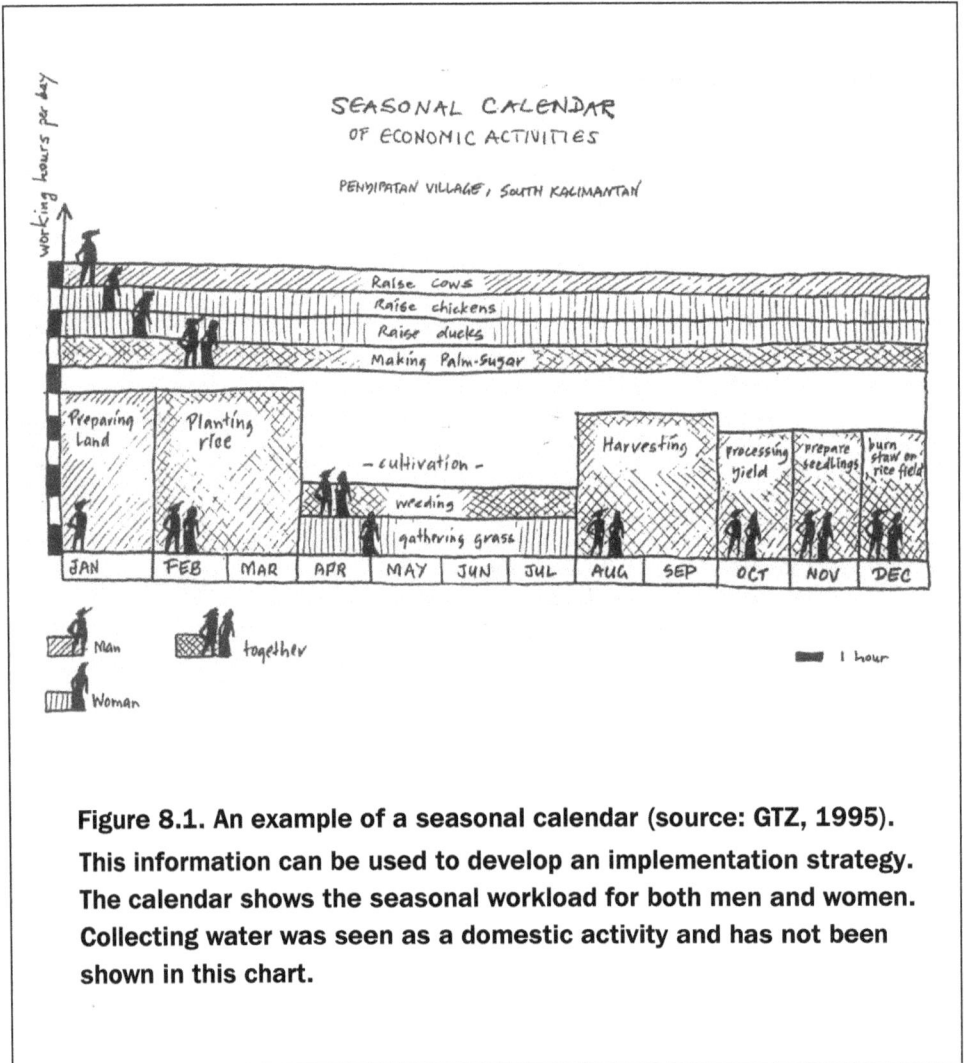

Figure 8.1. An example of a seasonal calendar (source: GTZ, 1995).

This information can be used to develop an implementation strategy. The calendar shows the seasonal workload for both men and women. Collecting water was seen as a domestic activity and has not been shown in this chart.

8.4 Communications

Visiting the field at this stage is essential to develop an effective project communication strategy that facilitates dialogue between users and project staff. This is critically important if expressions of demand are to be used later on in the project. At the very least, project staff should be aware of all the communities located within the project area, where they are and how to reach them physically. It is especially important to identify smaller, informal or remote settlements that may not feature in secondary data.

The various socio-economic groups that exist within communities should also be identified, together with appropriate opportunities for dialogue. The latter should build on existing practices, such as people's attendance at a regular market, a mobile clinic or a pension day. Project staff should ensure that opportunities are identified which enable them to communicate with all sectors of the community, including women and the poor.

8.5 Reviewing potential options

Other than investigating the enabling environment and conducting an initial assessment of demand, the third demand related measure associated with project preparation is an option review. It is recommended at this stage because it may be very difficult to undertake once detailed planning has started in terms of time and resources required.

The concept of providing people with an appropriate and environmentally sustainable choice of options is central to meeting demand. Our research has shown that few project staff have the breadth of knowledge or experience to be able to offer these options. It therefore makes sense to build the capacity of the implementing organisation before detailed planning starts.

To initiate this process, project staff must be aware of the characteristics of a wide range of technical, management and financial options. This is not simply a question of 'knowing the technology' as described, for example, in a water supply textbook. Project staff should know the basic characteristics that are likely to influence people's decisions; the various inputs required to use and sustain an option; and the wider implications for the environment and other people living in the area.

Project staff can be encouraged to develop their own set of 'option fact sheets'. These can be based on data obtained during a field assessment and, if necessary, a resulting review of potential options. The process itself builds capacity and can provide the project team with a valuable resource.

An example of this comes from the Kalahandi Water and Development Project in Orissa, undertaken by Save the Children Fund UK (Box 8.1). In this case the information collected was limited to technical options, but it provided the project team with the knowledge and skills to offer people a choice of service levels.

Box 8.1.   The Kalahandi Water and Development Project - technical review

The Kalahandi Water and Development Project, supported by Save the Children Fund (UK), was originally designed as a poverty focused but largely supply driven project. One of its objectives was to improve access to safe water in some of the most remote areas in the District.

The project focus was initially on boreholes and hand pumps, but this did not reflect the practical, financial and institutional difficulties of sustaining these options. Following a rapid appraisal conducted in 80 villages, it became evident that the local population faced a range of problems. This led to a review of technical options.

The aim of the review was to develop a portfolio of generic solutions that could be developed locally. Protected wells, filter wells, hand pumps, rain-water harvesting, borehole rehabilitation, drilling techniques and in-house treatment options were all investigated. Visits were made to adjoining districts and states, whilst additional work focused on determining capital and recurrent costs. The final document became a valuable source of information for the activities that followed.

In retrospect, what was missing was insight into people's priorities, perceptions and coping strategies. This reinforces the point that a technical review cannot be completed in isolation but must be based on a basic knowledge of demand, in terms of people's preferences and the type of contribution they may be willing to make in return.

8.6 Obtaining donor approval

The completion of a project strategy provides an early opportunity for a donor or an intermediary to review a project proposal and confirm or withdraw its support. This approval should not be confused with the later appraisal of a detailed community plan, which may involve users demonstrating their support for the proposed activities and how they are to be implemented. The following table gives some idea of the demand-related criteria that could be used by a donor to review a project strategy.

Table 8.2. Possible demand based criteria for donor approval

Factor	Key Issues
Information	Is the proposal informed by initial indications of demand for improved services, for example, based on a study of coping strategies?
Capacity	Does the implementing organisation have the capacity to use demand effectively and identify, develop and offer service options capable of meeting user demand?
	Do project staff have the skills, resources and time to stimulate demand if it is weak?
	Which indicators of demand will be used and when are they to be used?
Partnerships	Have partnerships been established which will enable demand to be met or managed in the future once implementation is completed?
Objectives and time-frame	Are objectives compatible with existing priorities and policies? Are they achievable within the stated time frame, taking into account the need for capacity building and need for users to make key decisions and any need to stimulate demand?
Communications	Is there a project communication strategy based on the need to initiate and maintain a dialogue with all users?
Inclusion	Have specific arrangements been made to identify and target marginalised groups and ensure their inclusion in the project process?
Risks	Have risks been identified and assessed, and how will they be shared?
Quality	How will the quality of the project's process, including facilitated decision-making, be measured and maintained?

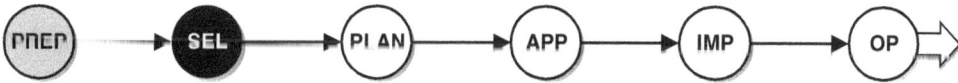

9. Selecting where and when to work

As previously mentioned, many projects involve a number of communities, each one of which may be associated with a sub-project. Limited resources, and the need to develop the capacity of the project team and its partners, may result in the project being implemented in phases. In this case, work has to be prioritised and communities selected. One of the criteria that could be used is demand.

In some cases, project staff are not responsible for prioritising sub-projects and selecting communities. For example, the decision may already have been made by local government. Alternatively, the project may involve only one community. Even in these circumstances, project staff should understand how activities could be proiritised, taking into account demand.

If expressions of demand are to be used to select communities or households in this way, it is important to recognise five potential problems:

1. Expressions of demand are only reliable if people have been informed of the implications of participating in a project. This requires that information is made accessible to all decision-makers.

2. Demand may be tempered by the fact that the credibility of the project team is untested and that the benefits may not be realised for several years. Past experience of poor water supply and sanitation projects may reduce demand in some communities.

3. Communities and households must have the opportunity to express whether or not they want to participate in a project. This may be difficult to arrange in remote areas or if people lack literacy skills.

4. Initial expressions of demand are more likely to come from those with influence or better access to information, and may not represent collective demand. They may also hide tensions within the community.

5. If demand is to be used in this way, the selection process itself must be transparent to avoid accusations of bias that could seriously undermine the credibility of a project team.

Despite these points, expressions of demand remain an important factor in selecting where to work and should not be overlooked. Three practical measures can be taken to ensure that expressions of demand are effective and these are described below.

1. Develop a project communication strategy

A project communication strategy should be developed and put into effect. This could be based on the results of investigations undertaken during project preparation. The strategy should be based on initiating and sustaining an effective dialogue with all potential users.

The most effective communication strategies may use several 'channels' and methods, reflecting the diversity of individuals and households found in every community. Specific measures may be needed to reach the most remote areas and marginalised groups within communities. Special effort may be needed to reach women, who are often socially or culturally excluded from receiving information and decision-making.

2. Ensure transparency

It is necessary to be completely transparent about the selection process. The criteria to be used for selection should be agreed by project stakeholders, including legitimate representatives of the communities in the project area.

3. Identify appropriate indicators of demand

Indicators of demand for project selection should be identified during project preparation. The following could be used:

- Observations of people's coping strategies, including the indicators of demand described in Section 8.2.1.

- The completion and return of an application form which specifically requires those completing it to interact with individuals and households.

- The completion of a basic village map, showing the distribution of households and other features.

- The establishment of a project fund, possibly taking the form of a savings account in a local bank. Relatively small amounts of cash could be used to pay for all or part of a feasibility study.

- A village or street sanitation campaign, in which people dispose of domestic rubbish, clear drainage ditches and repair damaged water or sanitation facilities. This could be used as a demonstration of demand for improved environmental sanitation and serve as an indicator of collective organisation.

All but the first of these points may require a degree of facilitation or capacity building, and arrangements have to be made to provide this. Mvula Trust's selection criteria (Mvula Trust, 1996) includes the formation of water or sanitation committees. In practice this was often completed without people realising what was expected of each member. At the very least, this experience reinforces the need for an effective project communication strategy.

Project staff may be disappointed if expressions of demand are less than anticipated. Whilst this can suggest a problem with the project's communication strategy, it may also be the result of people having other priorities. Weak demand may also result from the poor performance of development projects in the area.

Demand is not the only factor that can be used to select projects. Depending on the context, other criteria should also be considered:

- Frequently, selection has to fit in with external priorities, for example, those of local government or those implicit in a regional development plan.

- Expressions of demand may be balanced by an external assessment of people's needs for essential services. This could be based on the information supplied in a project application form. It would be wise to investigate which communities are not expressing demand and why.

- Selection has to take into account the skills and resources available to plan and implement water supply and sanitation improvements. This delay working in 'difficult' areas until project staff are more familiar with their roles and responsibilities.

- It may be necessary to pre-select certain communities in order to pilot approaches or technologies that the project team is not familiar with.

- It is often wise to start working in an area where success is more likely to reinforce the credibility of the process and the project team itself.

Ultimately, the best selection strategy is one that has emerged after considering all these factors and how they relate to the local context. An example of a selection strategy reflecting many of these points is described in Box 9.1.

Box 9.1. User participation in project selection

The Rural Drinking Water Supply and Sanitation Project, supported by the Government of Kenya and the Netherlands, started in Nyanza Province in 1983. Now at the end of its current phase, project staff have investigated ways to improve project selection. This has resulted in the development of a new approach. The approach has still to be tested, but it illustrates a number of important points.

During the preparation phase, a project's overall boundaries would be agreed in collaboration with government departments and other stakeholders. The size of the area would be constrained by the capacity of the project, but could include 30 to 40 villages.

Two representatives from every village (a man and a woman) would be invited to a two day workshop in a central location. This would be timed to coincide with the period after the harvest when people are more likely to be available, avoiding religious festivals or cultural events. The project's rules and methodology would be carefully explained, including the criteria for village selection.

The representatives would then receive training in order to be able to complete a project proposal form. This would require the collection of household data as well as information about water sources and the village's health status. This suggests that the representatives selected would have to be literate, a possible constraint in many rural areas. Post boxes would be established in convenient locations to facilitate the collection of the forms by an agreed date.

Expressions of demand (indicated by a completed application form) would be balanced with other considerations based on the information received. In this case, no cash contribution would be required.

Before this approach could be implemented, it would be necessary to check that some villages are not being excluded because the invitation does not reach them, or it cannot be understood. It would also be useful to investigate which villages did not submit an application form and why.

Toot (2000)

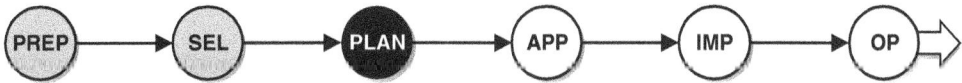

10. Developing a community plan

The next stage in the project process is to develop a community plan that sets out the activities to be undertaken at community level. This does not only involve the production of a detailed technical design. Management and contribution systems must also be developed that will later be used to implement a project and sustain it, once the project team withdraws.

The key point is to involve users in making informed decisions that will determine the type of service and facilities they receive. The process itself can be summarised in the form of a simple flow chart:

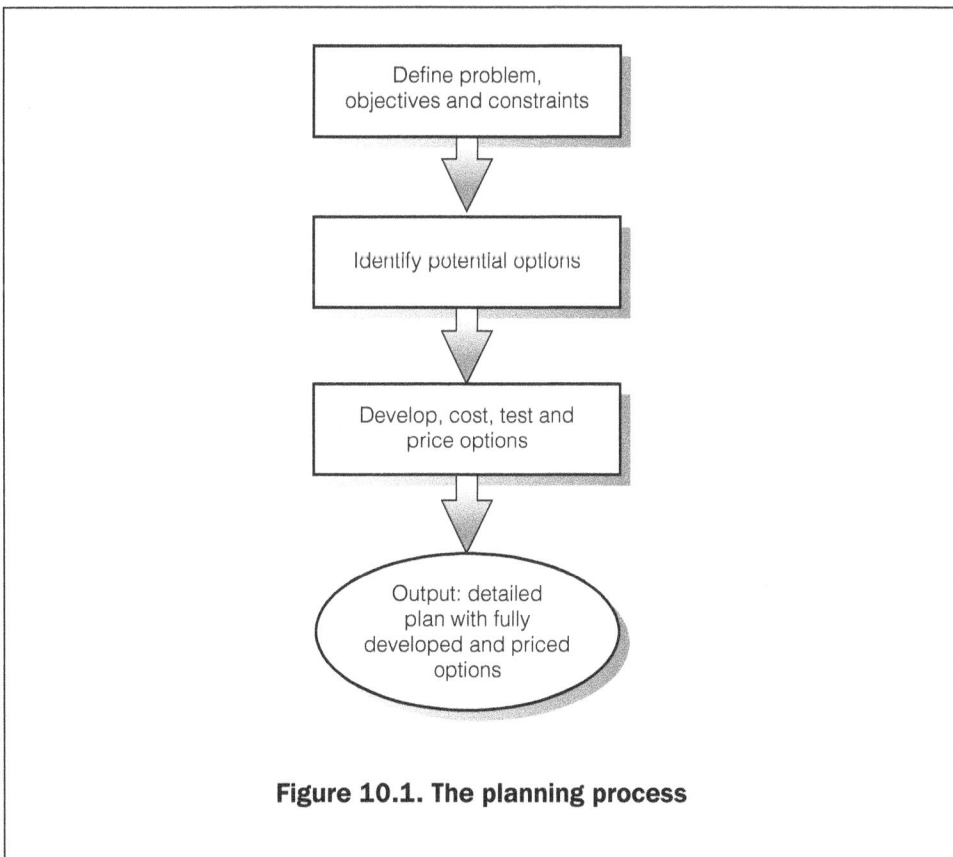

Figure 10.1. The planning process

If demand is to be reflected in the resulting plan, a constructive dialogue has to be maintained between users and project staff. Above all, this requires a conducive atmosphere based on mutual understanding and trust, and a pro-active approach to involving women and the poor in the planning process.

10.1 Defining the problem

Before appropriate options with the potential to meet demand are identified, project staff must understand why improved services are wanted in the first place. Local objectives have to be established.

This process is not always as 'bottom-up' as it sounds. It is often the case that people must be informed of the potential opportunities and associated benefits that could result. Achieving this, without imposing an external view or poten-tial solution can be difficult. An exposure visit to a completed project, with 'delegates' discussing the impact of the interventions made with the hosting community, is one possibility.

At this stage it is important that project staff do not confuse objectives with solutions. People often have a wealth of untapped information and ideas. However, they are rarely familiar with the full range of potential options or limiting factors. Problems can be defined, however, by facilitating people to analyse their own situation.

Among the various tools that can be used to do this, the following are particularly useful: *focus groups, participatory mapping, problem trees, objective trees and attribute ranking.*

10.1.1 Using focus groups

However uniform they may seem from the outside, most communities have a complex structure, made up of groups identified by factors such as gender, age, religion, wealth, ethnicity, clan and caste. Each group may have its own set of perceptions and priorities. The structure of a community may be revealed using a number of techniques, triangulating the results[14] to ensure that no group is excluded.

To ensure that the decisions made reflect the interests of all users, *focus groups* can be formed, their composition based on the results of previous investigations (and quite possibly participatory mapping as well). This can encourage the participation of people who may lack the confidence or credibility to discuss issues in a wider forum.

What is a focus group?

A small group of people made up of individuals sharing similar social, cultural or economic status, brought together with a facilitator to explore a particular issue. An example may be a group of women from a particular caste.

The use of focus groups enables perceptions and priorities to be explored in an informal, confidence building environment, with less risk that the process is dominated by an elite.

In some cases it is possible to use a group that already exists in a community, rather than attempt to establish something new, as long as this is appropriately constituted.

Focus groups are only as effective as the quality of their facilitation. The tendency for discussions to be dominated by one or two people, or led in a certain direction by a facilitator, must be checked. At some stage it will be necessary and desirable to bring different opinions together and achieve a degree of consensus. Focus groups can help achieve this by reinforcing the confidence and credibility of individuals to participate in decision-making.

---

[14] This means cross checking the results of one exercise with others to identify and rule out bias. Triangulation is an important principle used to validate the results of an investigation.

10.1.2 Participatory mapping

One of the more useful and adaptable tools that can be used by social facilitators (and indirectly by engineers) is a participatory map - a map or model representing a community, whether this is a rural settlement or a number of streets in a peri-urban area, often including the surrounding neighbourhood. The map is created by a number of people using materials and techniques with which they are familiar.

Participatory mapping can help identify marginalised households and in particular the 'invisible' poor who may not otherwise be identified as project stakeholders at all. Informal settlements, low caste hamlets and individual households may be particularly vulnerable because they have little or no voice to express their demand (see Box 10.1).

To identify the poorest of the poor, a social facilitator may have to probe deeply, combining a number of participatory techniques to ensure they are not being excluded.

Box 10.1.   Exclusion of a low caste hamlet in Madhya Pradesh, India

Banjaridhana is a hamlet of 56 low caste (harijan) households, situated within a kilometre of Sohapur, a larger and wealthier village. Many harijan work in fields owned by Sohapur residents, and Banjaridhana is administratively and politically part of Sohapur.

Banjaridhana was inadvertently excluded from a poverty focused water and sanitation project in Sohapur. UNICEF staff monitoring the project were unaware of the existence of the hamlet until an innocent question was asked by a harijan during a community meeting. The NGO implementing the project knew of the hamlet, but was keen to focus activities in Sohapur, where tangible results could be achieved more quickly.

Deverill and Wedgwood (2001)

Another use for maps of this sort could be to identify or clarify existing facilities and practices. For example, traditional water points, defaecation areas, rubbish pits and households with pit latrines can all be identified. Such features can be used to initiate dialogue. This can help establish a common understanding of the situation within a community. The quality of this dialogue is as important as the map itself. As with focus groups, engineers can derive a wealth of information from mapping exercises and need to involve themselves either directly or indirectly.

An example of a village map is shown in Figure 10.2. This is taken from a paper on participatory mapping by Neela Mukherjee (1992), published in an IIED publication on the Applications of Wealth Ranking (IIED, 1992). The map in Figure 10.2 details field boundaries and irrigation wells, suggesting a male point of view. In practice, a map drawn by women may be very different from that drawn by men, reflecting different priorities and perceptions. It is important to understand both male and female perceptions, reinforcing the usefulness of gender-segregated focus groups.

The mappers have also ranked households in terms of wealth, using criteria they defined themselves. The poorest households included those headed by widows with few assets, no land, no regular source of income, and not enough to eat throughout the year. Better off groups had more land and fewer dependants. Those in the more wealthy groups were also able to benefit from official income generating projects.

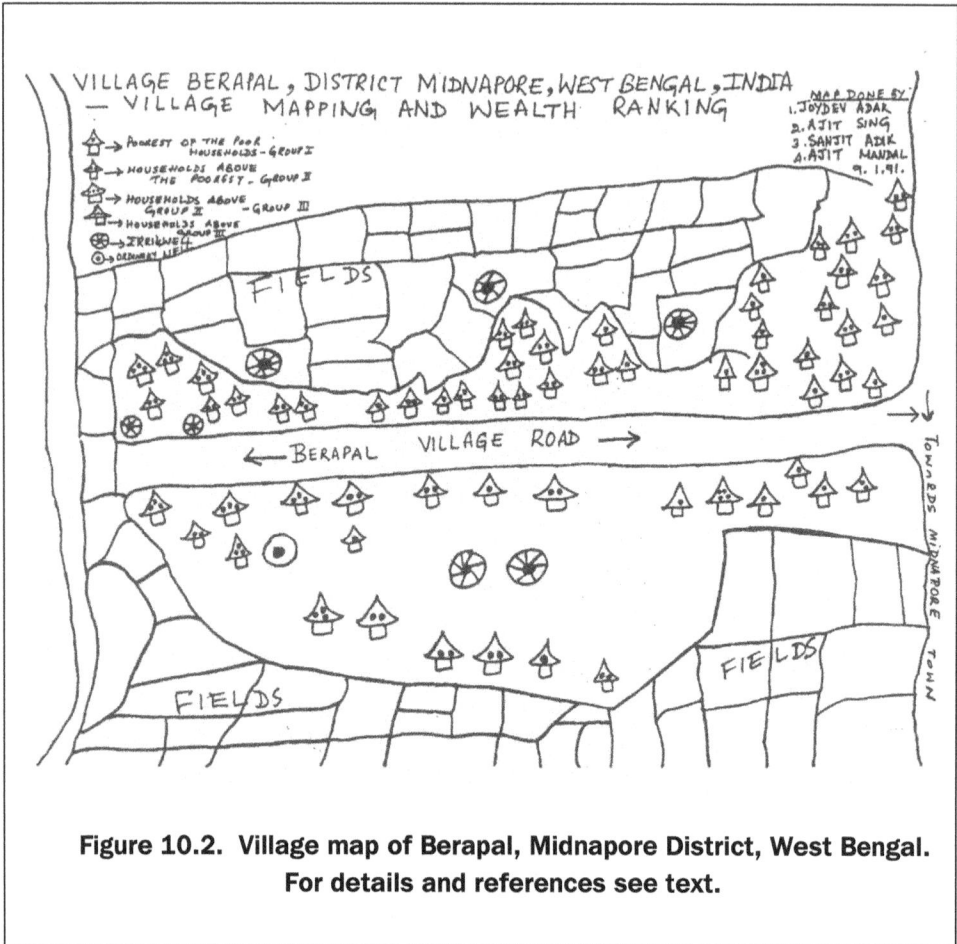

**Figure 10.2. Village map of Berapal, Midnapore District, West Bengal.
For details and references see text.**

If surveys focus on the area within a community's boundaries, information about neighbouring communities, surrounding resources and communication routes is not revealed and is therefore not discussed. Peripheral information of this type may be very important. For example it can help identify:

- Out-of-village areas used for refuse or excreta disposal by certain sections of the community.

- Additional water sources (and their ownership).

- The location of 'downstream' users dependent on water supplies within the village.

- The location of a school or clinic that could be incorporated within the project boundary.

- Marginalised communities, such as the harijan community described in Box 10.1.

- The possibilities for a multi-village scheme that may benefit from economies of scale.

10.1.3 Problem trees

The third participatory tool to be described is designed to identify problems (as perceived by a community), rank these in terms of their importance, and investigate how they are related. Represented graphically, the result of this exercise is called a problem tree, reflecting its branched appearance.

The creation of a problem tree needs careful facilitation in order to keep its size manageable. It is equally important that the facilitator does not lead the exercise, by concentrating on a particular issue when those participating have other concerns.

The use of focus groups to build their own problem trees can help a trained facilitator understand the diversity of opinion within a community. Shared concerns can also be identified and a mutually acceptable solution established.

Putting it together
The process of creating a problem tree is relatively simple. A group of people, typically six to twelve, is to record the problems they face on card or other material. Symbols can be agreed if people cannot write. The results are then sorted, with similar problems being grouped together. The causes and effects of each problem are then discussed. This can lead to additional cards being added and some being discarded. Finally, the problem cards are arranged to show their interrelationships.

When the group is happy with the result and agree that it represents their collective perceptions, the cards are stuck down and lines drawn to show the links between them. An example of a problem tree is shown in Figure 10.3.

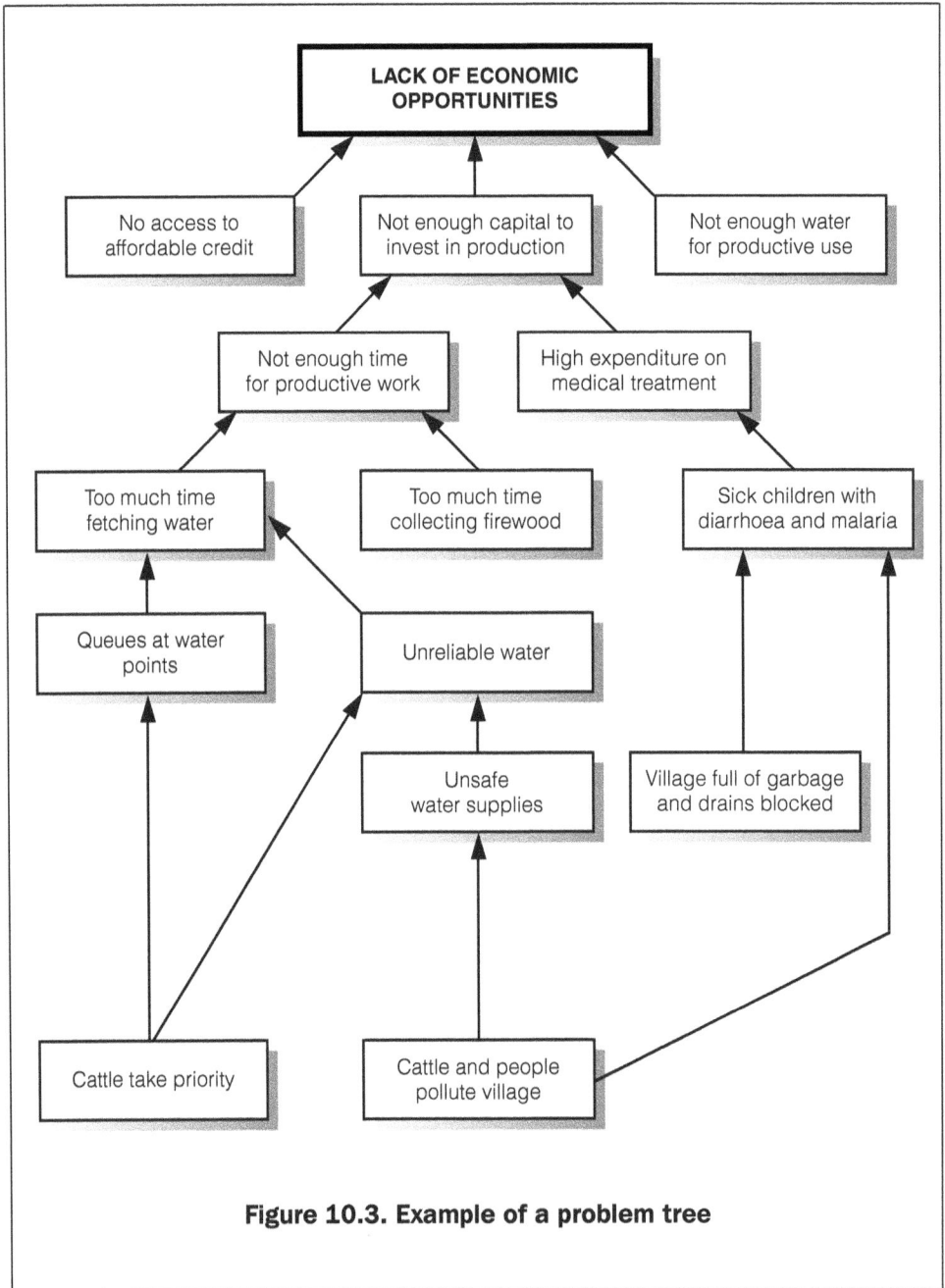

Figure 10.3. Example of a problem tree

10.1.4 Objective trees

It is a relatively simple exercise to transform a problem statement into an objective, simply by rewording or rephrasing it. In the same way, a problem tree can be transformed into an objective tree[15].

This transformation can be a very useful exercise. Firstly, it links the problems people face with the decisions they will make. Involving people in decision-making is only likely to be effective if those decisions are felt to be relevant. Secondly, it can help project staff appreciate the breadth of activities that need to be undertaken to achieve a significant impact. Lastly, the exercise high-lights the constraints that all projects face and introduces a certain amount of reality into the process - it is unlikely that every objective can be addressed.

An example of an objective tree is shown in Figure 10.4. This is based on the preceding problem tree. The shaded objectives are those which have not been incorporated into a water and sanitation project. It is important to note that both problem and objective trees require a high standard of facilitation, ensuring that people have sufficient information to link cause and effect.

Figures 10.3 and 10.4 reflect water supply, sanitation and hygiene. Logic suggests that interventions should be integrated. This can be achieved in two ways. Separate 'stand alone' water, sanitation and hygiene initiatives could be planned together and their implementation co-ordinated. Alternatively, two or all of these components could be packaged into a single project. One fre-quently encountered problem associated with packages of this sort is that hygiene and sanitation are seen as 'bolt-on components' and are frequently marginalised. For more details, see Section 7.2.

---

[15] An alternative way of building an objective tree is described in Toolkits, published by Save the Children Fund. For further details see Gosling and Matthews (1995).

```
                    ┌─────────────────────────────┐
                    │     IMPROVE ECONOMIC        │
                    │     OPPORTUNITIES           │
                    └─────────────────────────────┘
```

IMPROVE ECONOMIC OPPORTUNITIES

Providing saving and credit scheme

Increase amount of capital for investment

Develop new water sources and improve water use efficiency

Increase time for productive work

Reduce expenditure on medical treatment

Reduce water collection time

Grow more firewood

Reduce incidence of diarrhoea and malaria

Increase number of water points

Increase amount of water available

Improve water quality

Clean up village and restore drains

Provide alternative water supplies for cattle

Prevent cows entering village

Encourage people to use toilets

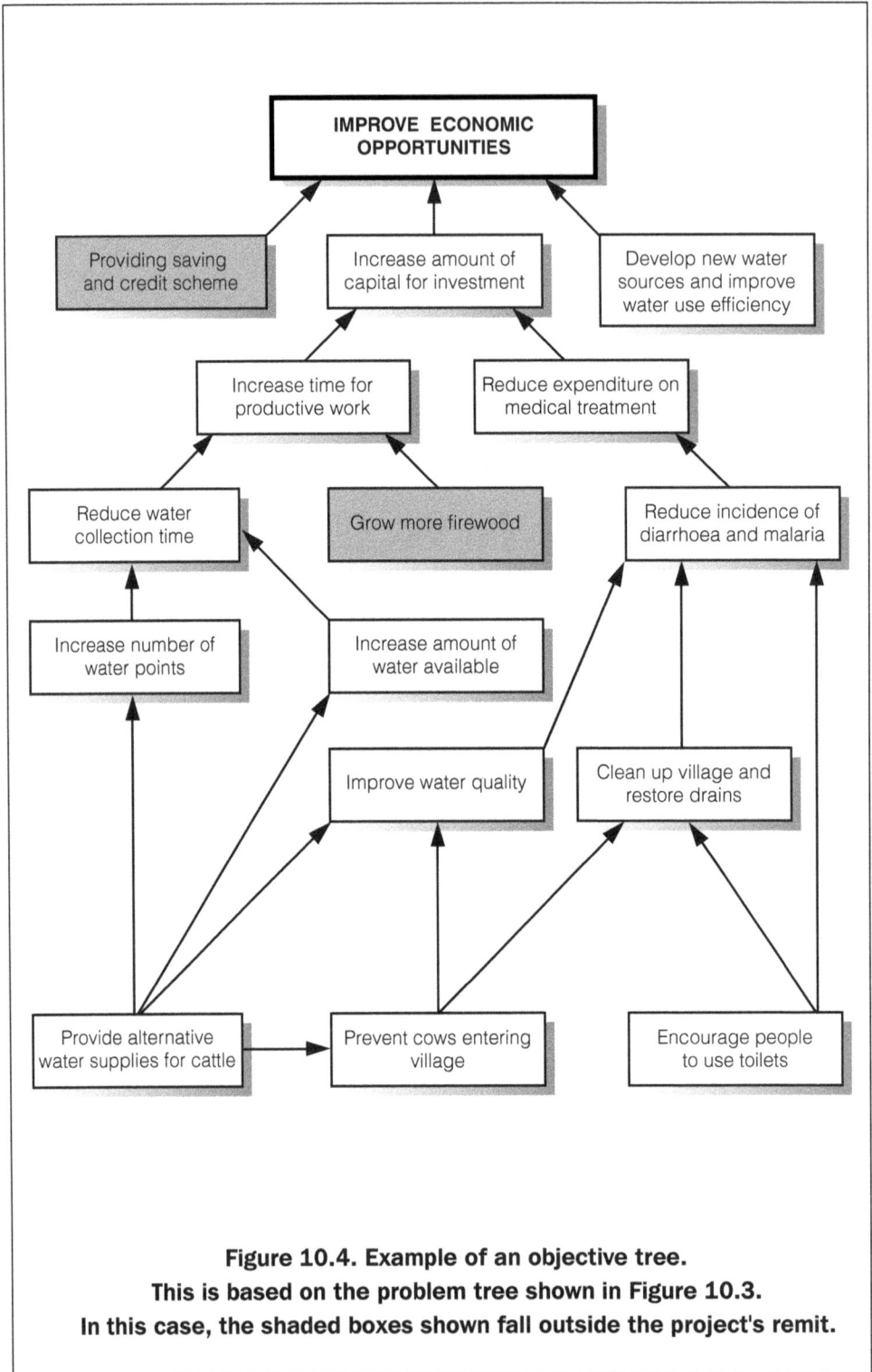

Figure 10.4. Example of an objective tree.
This is based on the problem tree shown in Figure 10.3.
In this case, the shaded boxes shown fall outside the project's remit.

10.1.5 Attribute ranking

So far, the tools described concern problems and objectives. The desired characteristics (or attributes) of a service or a related facility have still not been clearly identified. It is important that this is done, because household demand is largely dependent on this factor.

One way of achieving this is by attribute ranking. Participants are encouraged to first identify and discuss the attributes of an improved service or facility. Dialogue can be initiated by introducing a wide range of characteristics, each represented on a card. These are then discussed and sorted into three piles - 'desirable', 'undesirable' and 'unsure'. If necessary, participants can suggest new cards.

The final ranking is then scored to judge their relative importance, using a simple technique such as pocket chart voting[16]. The exercise can be made more sophisticated (and more complicated) by getting participants to score an existing facility first. An example is shown in Figure 10.5. In practice, symbols rather than words could be used to describe each attribute.

---

[16] Pocket chart voting is a technique in which participants can express a preference by placing a marker (such as a bean) in a pocket associated with a particular attribute.

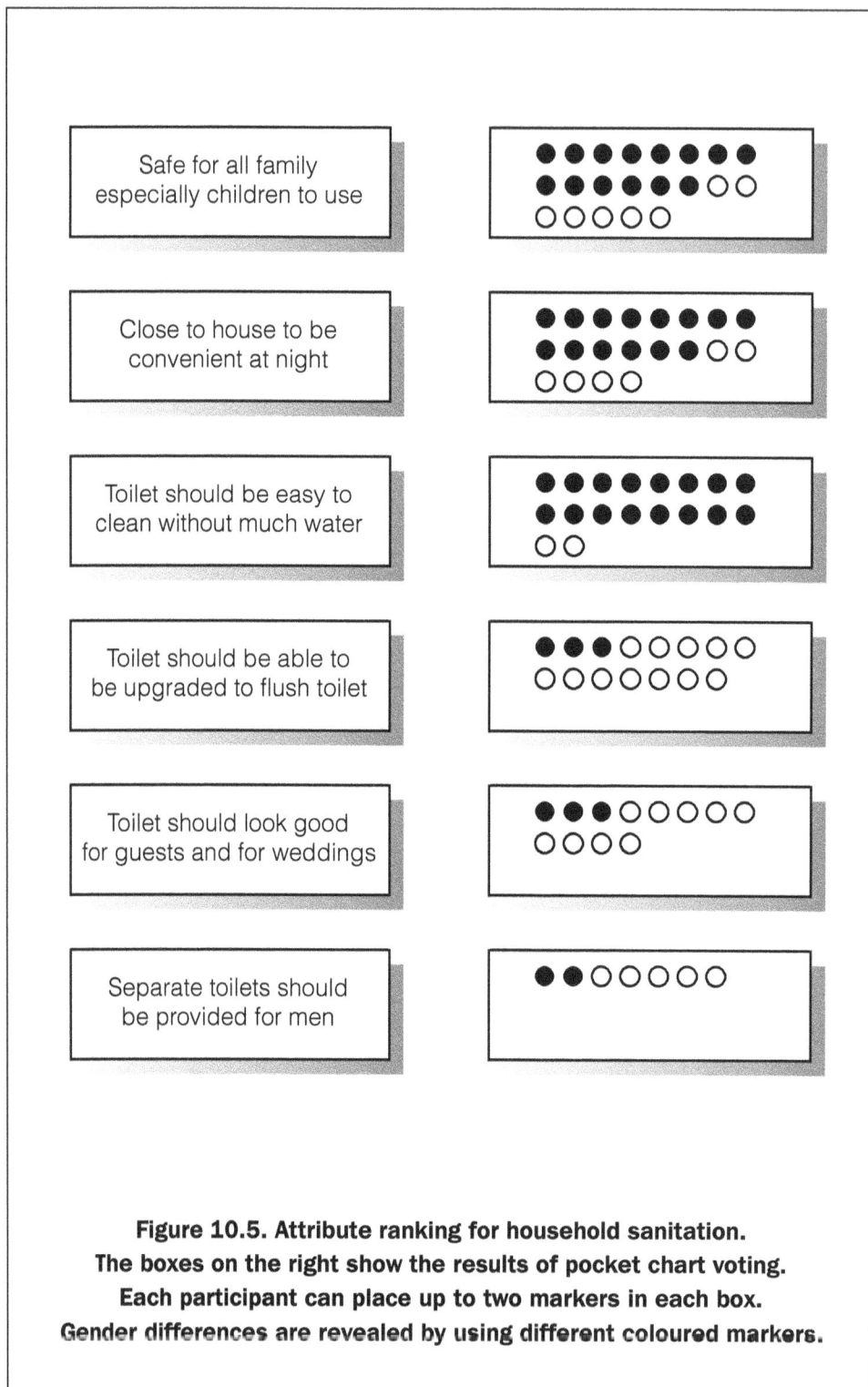

Safe for all family especially children to use	●●●●●●●●●● ●●●●●●●○○ ○○○○○
Close to house to be convenient at night	●●●●●●●●● ●●●●●●●○○ ○○○○
Toilet should be easy to clean without much water	●●●●●●●●●● ●●●●●●●●● ○○
Toilet should be able to be upgraded to flush toilet	●●●○○○○○○ ○○○○○○○
Toilet should look good for guests and for weddings	●●●○○○○○○ ○○○○
Separate toilets should be provided for men	●●○○○○○

**Figure 10.5. Attribute ranking for household sanitation.
The boxes on the right show the results of pocket chart voting.
Each participant can place up to two markers in each box.
Gender differences are revealed by using different coloured markers.**

In conjunction with the other tools described, attribute ranking provides project staff with sufficient detail to identify potential options which are likely to meet demand. This is the subject of the following section. First, however, it is necessary to consider how demand for sanitation can be stimulated.

Stimulating demand for sanitation

So far in this booklet, sanitation has been treated in much the same way as water supply. However, whereas demand for improved water supply is often very apparent (the main issue being how to respond to it), demand for sanitation often seems to be weak or even non-existent.

The following four pages explain:

■ Why does demand for sanitation often seem weak?

■ What does stimulating demand mean in practice?

■ PHAST – a method of developing the link between health, hygiene and sanitation.

Why does demand for sanitation often seem weak?

There may be several reasons why demand for sanitation seems weak. Based on the experience of those involved in developing these guidelines, important factors may include the following:

- Sanitation is often presented to people as a health issue although potentially it has other benefits which may be valued more highly.

- People may find it difficult to make the link between how they dispose of their excreta and related diseases with which they have lived for generations.

- Sanitation practices are long established and frequently have social, cultural, religious, livelihood or aesthetic dimensions that are not appreciated by project staff.

- People are unaware of the potential for effective sanitation to improve their lives. This may be reinforced by the often dismal conditions of the facilities they have experienced.

- Political support for sanitation is weak compared to water supply. One reason is that sanitation benefits are focused at household rather than at community level and are less visible as a result.

- Limited access to sanitation hardware and related information on the options may be obstructing demand.

- Sanitation can be relatively expensive in terms of the investment required. Other demands can take priority and may have to be satisfied first.

Project staff must understand these issues, and be responsive to them, if demand for sanitation is to be stimulated or 'unlocked'.

What does stimulating demand mean in practice?

Based on the experience of the organisations involved in developing these guidelines, the following measures can prove very effective in stimulating demand.

- Understand and respond to people's priorities. This may mean dealing with water supply first, together with other activities such as hygiene promotion needed to meet project objectives.

- Establish the qualities people value, and reflect this in the options offered. In this respect, men and women's perceptions of convenience, comfort, security, privacy, health benefits and status may all be important.

- Think in terms of incremental change, and ensure that there is sufficient time in which people's perceptions and behaviour can be modified. Experience shows this can take 5 to 10 years. In the limited time available it maybe possible to 'seed' demand across the project area. See Box 10.2 for details.

- Develop an appropriate range of sanitation options which reflects the diversity of demand present in a community. Upgradable options allow people to respond to future changes in their demand as their perceptions change.

- Build understanding of the links between safe sanitation, hygiene and health. In this respect, the use of PHAST[17] tools can be highly effective - if used to encourage learning and action rather than as teaching aids.

- Make sanitation more affordable. Make use of local knowledge, skills and resources. Consider establishing a revolving fund or micro-credit scheme. A limited, well-targeted subsidy may be needed to help those with less access to financial resources provided that this is a response to demand.

- Ensure that people know about the sanitation programme and have access to information and hardware. The private sector may have a role to play, supplying sanitation long after project staff have left.

---

[17] PHAST: Participatory Hygiene and Sanitation Transformation. See next page for details.

Box 10.2. Stimulating demand for sanitation: the Mbila Sanitation and hygiene project, KwaZulu Natal

Mbila is a relatively isolated tribal ward in northern KwaZulu Natal, consisting of ten rural communities, each of about 100 Zulu households. In 1998 it was decided by the Mvula Trust to start a sanitation project in the area, based on a earlier pilot project which had finished some years previously. A sanitation committee was duly appointed by the tribal authority. Partners in Development was appointed as the implementing organisation.

The sanitation committee choose to initiate the project in all ten communities, despite the fact that this would add to logistic problems (and costs) and that, in the first phase of the project, only 200 latrine subsidies were available. Each of these was worth 600 Rand (then worth about 1,00 US $).

Learning important lessons from the previous project, it was decided to offer a number of superstructure options sharing a Ventilated Improved Pit (VIP) design. The subsidy was used to sink and line a pit and supply a vent pipe, pit cover and pedestal (the VIP and seat is an established norm throughout much of KwaZulu Natal). The prospective owner was responsible for completing the superstructure according to his or her preference. A catalogue was produced detailing the various superstructure options and their approximate costs.

With only twenty latrine subsidies per community, draws were held in each area to determine who could apply. This mechanism, devised by the sanitation committee, was respected for its transparency and equity. Both the process and the completed latrines helped generate interest and demand from other households, as a result of which the programme has been expanded with additional funding.

Partners in Development (South Africa)

A householder stands in front of her recently completed latrine, complete with a relatively affordable and highly popular reed superstructure.

PHAST

PHAST (Participatory Hygiene and Sanitation Transformation) is a participatory technique that develops people's understanding of the linkages between sanitation, hygiene and health. The aim is to encourage participants to plan their own sanitation and hygiene initiatives, both at household and at community level.

The technique uses a number of graphical tools such as the sanitation ladder described in Section 10.3.2. It relies on quality facilitation. The risk is that the tools are used to instruct people, removing the opportunity for them to learn from and act on their own experience.

WEDC/Darren Saywell

Above - men meet to dicuss their plans.
Before the opinions of each group are consolidated,
women would meet separately.

For details about PHAST see the Water and Sanitation Programme (Africa region) website: www.wsp.org. A video 'Healthy Communities' documenting the process is now available from this source.

10.2 Identifying potential options

Having established people's objectives and the attributes of an improved service, the identification of options with the potential to meet demand can be a relatively simple process. The factors that should be taken into account are shown in Figure 10.6. At this stage, it is not necessary to develop potential options into actual solutions.

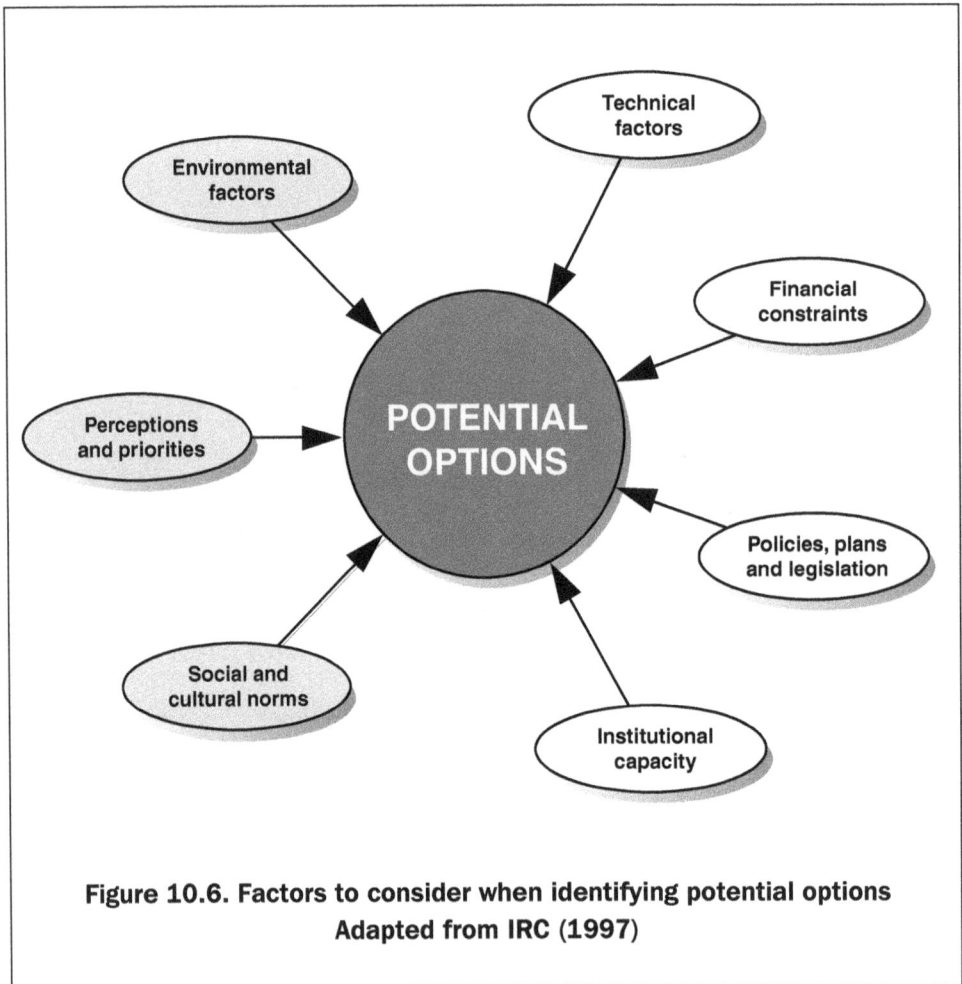

Technical factors

Environmental factors

Financial constraints

Perceptions and priorities

POTENTIAL OPTIONS

Policies, plans and legislation

Social and cultural norms

Institutional capacity

Figure 10.6. Factors to consider when identifying potential options
Adapted from IRC (1997)

A number of principles can be used to guide the identification process, and some of these are suggested below.

1. Investigate current practices and underlying perceptions

In terms of impact and sustainability, it is often more effective to develop current practices rather than introduce an 'alien' technology. It may be possible to introduce improvements to water supplies and sanitation incrementally, keeping pace with (but not exceeding) the capacity of users to sustain them.

2. Ensure that the project team has adequate knowledge

Ensure that technical staff are familiar with (i) a broad range of technologies and their characteristics, and (ii) the potential for each option to be developed to provide a range of service levels. This reinforces the value of conducting a technical review referred to in Section 8.5.

3. Consider technical options

Start by identifying potential technical options. Appropriate management and contribution systems can be 'added on' to complement technology during the following stage.

4. Participatory investigation

Conduct field investigations with (rather than for) people. One indicator of demand is the extent to which potential users are prepared to investigate potential options, for example, by digging trial pits or using a shallow auger to find a local water table. In some cases it may be possible for people to plan their own investigation, with project staff adopting a more advisory role.

5. Match attributes

Compare the characteristics of potential options with the attributes of what users want, taking into account constraints that may reduce choice. Objective tree and attribute ranking can both be used to guide this process. At this stage, rank rather than rule out options.

6. Be transparent.

Not only should technologies be discussed with users, so should the risks and consequences of them failing. In particular this relates to ground water investigations, drilling (which may prove unsuccessful) and the possibility of the final plan not being approved by the project's funder.

7. Make the link

Do not overlook the links between water supply, sanitation and hygiene. For example, if latrines are to be provided and hygiene promoted, where will the water come from to use and clean them and who will undertake this task? If a pour flush latrine is preferred, this could amount to an additional 5-10 litres per person per day. Similarly, if house connections are to be provided, consumption will be higher and so too will be the volume of wastewater that needs to be disposed of or utilised.

8. Remember the environment.

This does not only apply to the direct issues of establishing the safe yield of a spring and ensuring wastes do not cause pollution, but also the potential impact of using natural resources on the environment and the people whose livelihoods depend on it. For example, if a significant amount of water is to be abstracted from a number of wells, conservation measures may be needed to sustain the water table.

10.3 Developing potential options into real options

Once potential options have been identified, they can be developed into services and facilities capable of meeting demand. Whilst it is important to reflect the perceptions and priorities of users in the final 'product', whatever is planned must also be environmentally sustainable, technically feasible, financially viable, institutionally supportable, socially acceptable and culturally sensitive!

As potential technical options are developed into a number of service levels (some may be discarded along the way), these can be complemented by appropriate management and contribution systems. This is shown schematically in Figure 10.7.

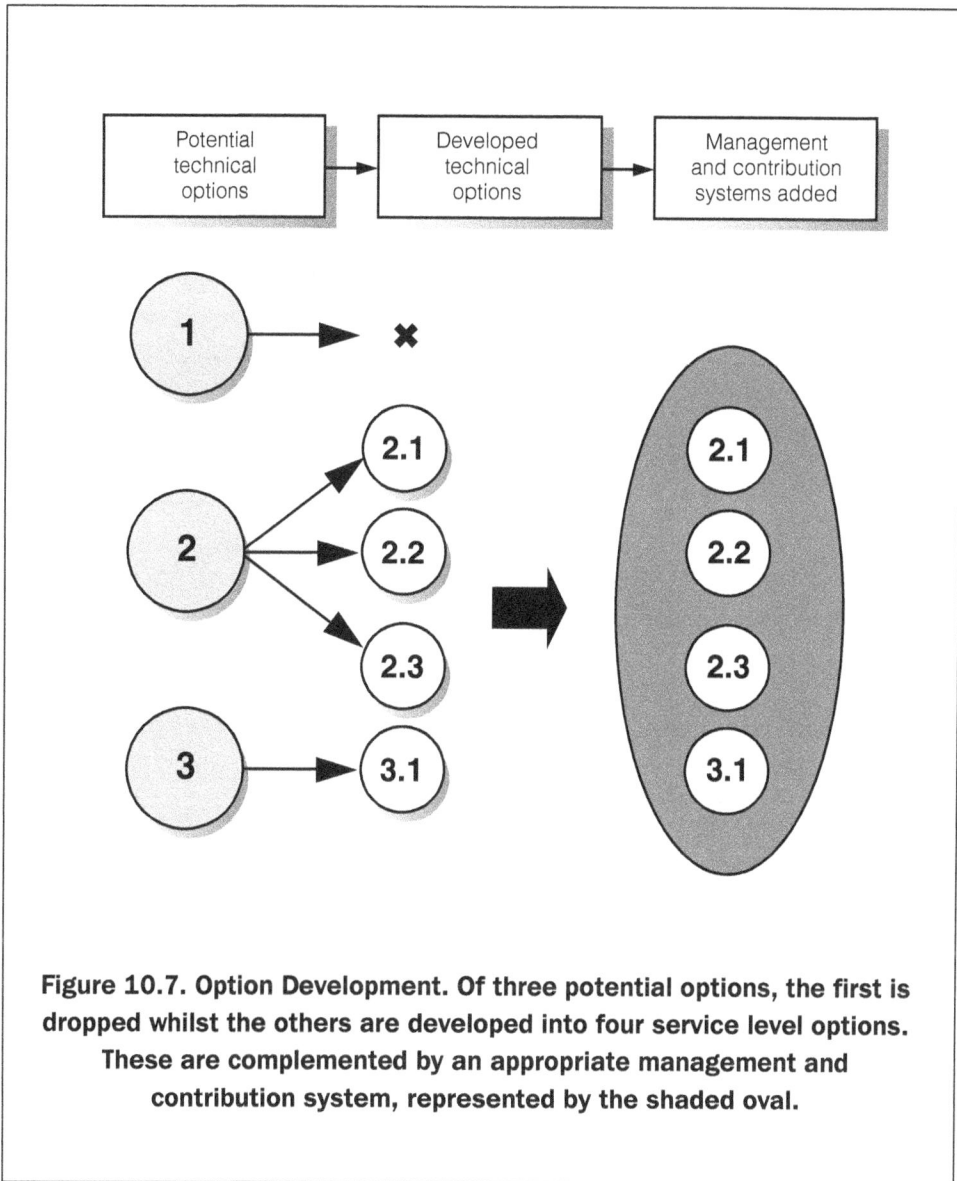

Figure 10.7. Option Development. Of three potential options, the first is dropped whilst the others are developed into four service level options. These are complemented by an appropriate management and contribution system, represented by the shaded oval.

Box 10.3 provides an example that illustrates how this pattern of option development could be reflected in practice. *This is linked to the process outlined in Figure 10.7.* The description is based on a real case study in KwaZulu Natal, South Africa, albeit with minor adaptations. In practice, technical options were developed over the course of the project to overcome the limitations of dug wells.

Box 10.3. Option development in practice: Ubombo Family Wells Programme, Maputaland, South Africa

The following example of option development is based on an actual scenario, taken from the Ubombo Family Wells Programme in KwaZulu Natal, South Africa.

In this case, three potential technical options have been identified: The numbers relate to those in Figure 10.7.

① A piped water supply from a nearby lake.
② Shallow wells.
③ Rain water harvesting.

As these are developed into practical options, it transpires that the cost of sustaining the piped water supply ① is much higher than anticipated. There are also doubts about the available local capacity to manage a piped water supply. After consulting with focus groups and the water committee, it is agreed to seek an alternative option.

The well option ② is investigated in more detail, resulting in three service levels associated with communal tube wells, family tube wells and dug wells. The latter are primarily intended to satisfy demand for horticulture and livestock. In some areas it is established that the water table is inaccessible, necessitating the development of a rain-water harvesting option ③.

The family tube well provides an alternative to households that could have afforded the piped water supply. This option has 'upgrade potential' and could be augmented with a solar pump and roof tank to provide an in-house connection, as long as waste water could be disposed of effectively.

During the development process, the water committee and focus groups are involved in the development of a management and contribution system.

The result of this process is a detailed plan, complete with a 'menu' of service level options. Demand for these could be tested before presenting the plan to the community in a mass meeting for their endorsement or rejection.

Many water supply projects are undertaken to improve people's health directly. There is however, strong evidence that the economic benefits which follow can also have a profound impact[18]. The time saved by women (because water is made more accessible) can be used for income generating activities. Many of these activities make use of the water provided.

This link has been recognised by many organisations including at least two in Nepal. The Rural Water Supply and Sanitation Fund Development Board (the Fund Board) has established a revolving savings and credit fund for each of its projects, allowing women's groups to start a business whether or not it is related to water supply. The income generated helps to sustain the water supply (see Box 10.4). In other areas of Nepal, the Gurkha Welfare Scheme is piloting drip irrigation systems. These are also proving very successful.

Box 10.4. The Women's Technical Support Service, Nepal

One of the objectives of the Fund Board in Nepal is to provide opportunities for income generation, focused on women in particular. The scheme has been very successful, demonstrated by the case of Bhatikharda village, where the local Women's Group have started a revolving fund for goat and pig rearing.

With support from the financial authority, at least twenty families have used the scheme, which has a 100% loan repayment record. Reflecting the success of the Women's Group, the village water users group has decided to give them responsibilities for managing the sanitation revolving loan fund, a second Fund Board initiative.

This example, by no means unique, illustrates the link between water and production. The link must be recognised if demand is to be captured. Additional inputs - such as capital for a revolving fund - may be needed.

---

[18] See for example the Looking Back study undertaken by WaterAid. For details see WaterAid (2001).

Economic enhancements such as those described in Box 10.4 do not necessarily benefit the poor. Instead, they may increase the poverty gap that exists between them and the better off. Specific measures must be taken to identify and help overcome the constraints which prevent the poor taking up opportunities of this sort.

10.3.1 User involvement in option development or in option testing?

Ensuring that users participate in the development of options is one way of capturing their demand. Alternatively, it is possible to test the demand for developed options, using an appropriate demand assessment technique to establish, amongst other things, the contribution that people are willing to make. Each approach has a number of advantages and disadvantages, and these are summarised in Table 10.1(a and b).

Table 10.1a. Involving users in the development of options	
Advantages	**Disadvantages**
Increased opportunities for dialogue between project staff and potential users. This may reinforce a relationship of mutual understanding and trust.	Process may not be truly representative: focus groups can be dominated by an elite, whilst only relatively small number of potential users can be involved.
Increased opportunities to identify, assess, use or adapt local knowledge, skills and systems.	Considerable time may be needed to discuss concepts and interpret perceptions.
Participatory process can identify important details that may have significant impact on demand.	Potential users themselves may not have time to be able to participate as required.
Participation may encourage a sense of ownership and acceptance of associated responsibilities.	
Participatory process can build capacity for a future role in managing the service provided.	

Table 10.1b. Testing demand for developed options	
Advantages	**Disadvantages**
Demand assessment techniques can provide information on what people are willing to pay for options. This helps design a pricing or tariff structure.	Potentially these techniques are less able to capture demand as the decision-making point occurs after a range of options has been developed.
Various demand assessment techniques are available which can be adapted to suit a number of situations.	Depending on methods used, can be expensive to implement and costly to make significant design changes if these are required.
Depending on method used, the demand assessment may be relatively rapid. This may be important for project staff and potential users.	May undermine the sense of ownership which is important for community management.
The process can be designed to capture opinions from different groups within a community with less risk of an elite dominating proceedings.	
Some methods are statistically robust, with the capacity to identify and rule out bias.	

In practice, the best solution may be to involve users in both the development of options and option testing using an appropriate form of demand assessment. Further details of demand assessment techniques that could be used in this way are described in Section 10.4.2.

10.3.2 Communicating ideas

Whether involved in development or testing, potential users must be fully informed of the characteristics, costs, benefits and risks associated with each option. Communicating ideas can be extremely difficult, especially if people have not been exposed to them before. A number of techniques can be used or adapted to help get messages across:

- Maps - superimposing a plan on a community map. These do not have to be on paper, but could be painted on a wall or floor.

- Visits to neighbouring projects where similar options have been developed. This includes dialogue with users and managers.

- Physical models of the proposed facilities. Cut-away models can help explain how facilities work and what is needed to maintain them.

- Pictures, photographs, 'picture stories' and videos. In this category are the water and sanitation ladders. These can be used to establish local perceptions and practices, promote a discussion about improvements, and stimulate demand and behavioural change (Figure 10.8).

- Role-plays and street theatre. These can be used to demonstrate how a management or contribution system could work.

- Demonstrations of service levels and facilities. These must be realistic and designed to illustrate how a technology could be used and its costs and benefits, rather than advocating a particular level of service.

- Demonstration facilities associated with sanitation production centres and rural sanitation markets, either run by a local NGO or a private entrepreneur.

- Attractive 'catalogues' or simple manuals illustrating different options, their characteristics and costs, and how to build or obtain them.

- The use of pie charts and other graphical tools to examine a contribution policy or tariff structure.

- Identifying, investigating and highlighting the positive steps taken by some individuals (positive deviants) to improve their access to water supply and sanitation.

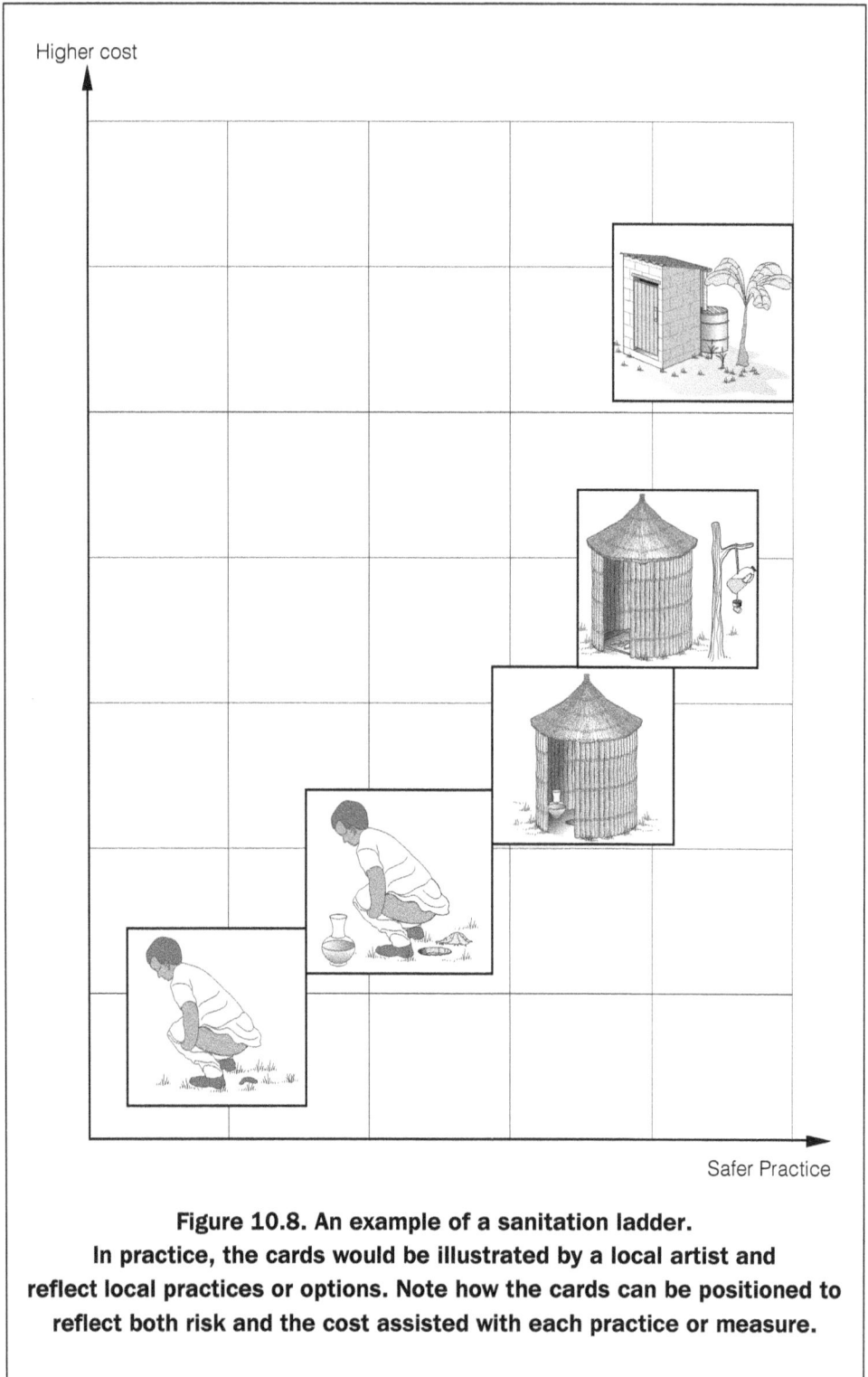

Higher cost

Safer Practice

Figure 10.8. An example of a sanitation ladder.
In practice, the cards would be illustrated by a local artist and
reflect local practices or options. Note how the cards can be positioned to
reflect both risk and the cost assisted with each practice or measure.

10.3.3 Meeting demand for higher service levels

Some implementing organisations seem reluctant to offer higher service levels for water and sanitation, even if demand exists and sufficient resources are available. This is often a question of ideology. Whilst it is not the purpose of these guidelines to advocate a particular point of view, the following issues should be borne in mind:

- The community's attitude to higher service levels must be established. In some cases, collective demand for a basic, equitable service must be satisfied before a community is willing to consider the introduction of higher service levels.

- Unmet demand may result in individuals developing their own coping strategies e.g. private boreholes. If there is competition for resources, this can destabilise a project and compromise its sustainability.

- In the case of water supply, project staff should first confirm if sufficient water resources are available to offer higher service levels, taking seasonal variations into account.

- The need to meet or manage future demand should be considered before offering higher service levels.

- The system must be considered as a whole, to ensure that the provision of higher service levels does not undermine the financial sustainability of lower service levels due to the inefficiency of implementing the latter on a reduced scale.

- Prices and other forms of contribution should reflect the cost of providing and sustaining the associated service level.

- The provision of higher service levels should increase the financial resources available to the scheme and may open up opportunities for cross subsidising the poor.

- If higher levels of service for water supply are to be provided, the associated issue of wastewater disposal should be addressed and reflected in the contributions required.

■ The use of intermediate service levels could be considered as a compromise if higher service levels are not to be implemented. These can often fill important gaps in a menu of options. An example is the supply of water to households using the trickle feed drum, described in Figure 10.9.

In many cases it may make sense for project staff to adopt an incremental approach to upgrading. This would have to be reflected in the project's overall strategy.

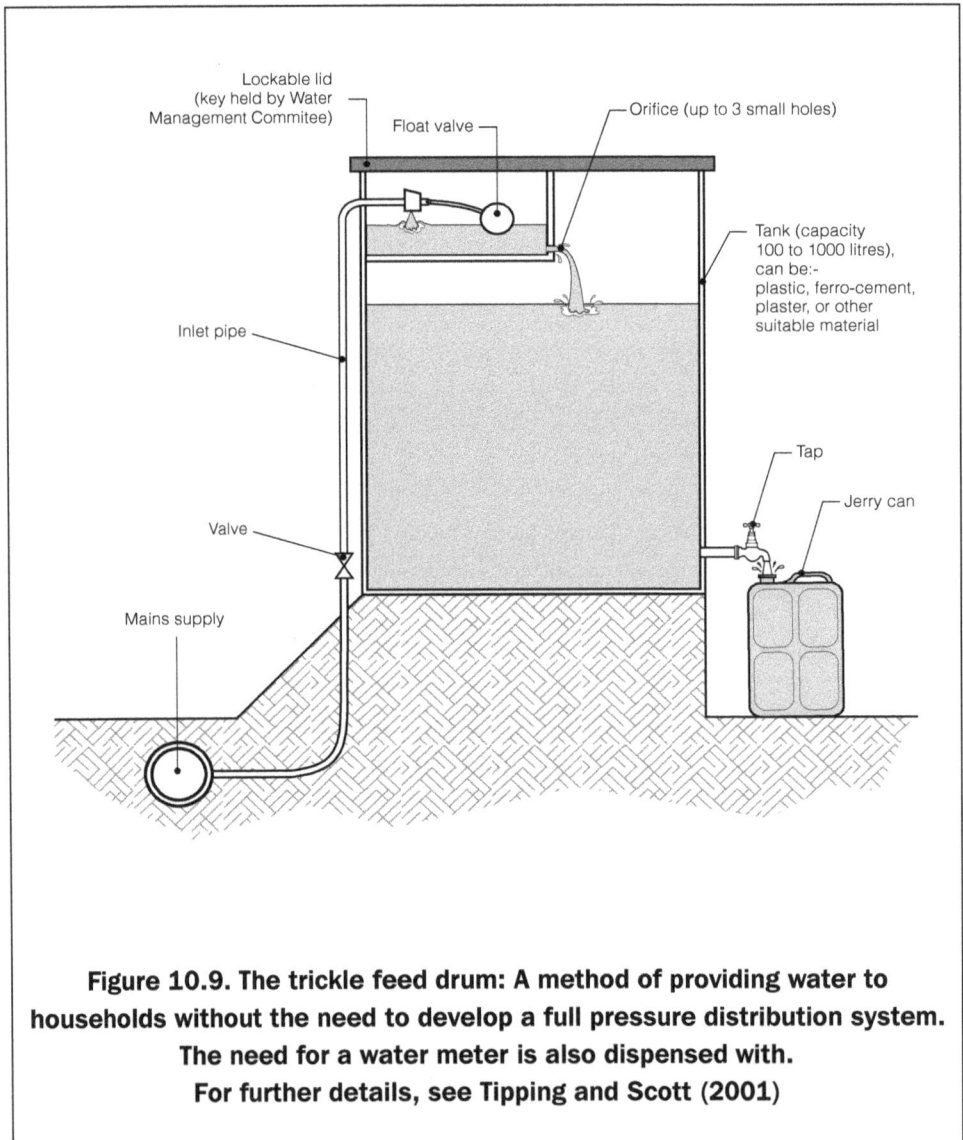

Figure 10.9. The trickle feed drum: A method of providing water to households without the need to develop a full pressure distribution system. The need for a water meter is also dispensed with. For further details, see Tipping and Scott (2001)

For example, a community could be provided with a basic water supply designed to satisfy initial demand, albeit with a degree of built-in upgradability. At this stage, any unmet demand for higher service levels would have to be controlled by the local management committee.

After a period of time, the project could be revisited by support staff. By this stage, users should be familiar with their current system and its capacity to provide for higher levels of service. Their knowledge could be reinforced by monitoring both supply and consumption. Upgrades could then be offered to the households that want them and are willing to pay the additional capital and recurrent costs.

10.3.4 Management and contribution systems

So far in this section the emphasis has been on the identification and development of appropriate technical options. It is also possible to extend the principle of user choice to management and contribution systems. Some issues arise:

1. Potential management and contribution options need to be identified before they can be developed. Local and regional policies and plans should be taken into account. It is suggested that project staff compile their own inventory of non-technical options, taking into account the existence of indigenous systems and local policies and plans.

2. The introduction of multiple service levels and associated contribution systems will add significantly to the responsibilities for local management. This should be reflected in capacity building and training. An incremental approach may be required.

3. Local management systems cannot operate in total isolation but inevitably need a degree of support from the responsible authority. The provision of higher service levels will increase this requirement.

4. Managers and their staff need incentives. An over reliance on volunteers has led to some local management organisations being short lived. In many countries this factor has contributed to the under achievement of water and sanitation projects.

5. Management can be significantly strengthened by legal recognition. It is often possible to register a water and sanitation committee with local government. A legitimate committee is also more likely to receive technical and managerial support from local government. Local disputes can be avoided by formalising the ownership of the water source.

6. Registered committees may be responsible to a local authority, potentially improving their transparency and accountability. For example, there could be a requirement to submit books to local government for annual audit.

7. A project can only have a single management system, reinforcing the need for an appropriate mechanism for collective decision-making. Checks may be required to prevent a powerful elite undermining or dominating management decisions. Traditional systems may be used or adapted if they are transparent, representative and accountable.

8. Options based on community management but which involve contracting out certain roles or services to the private sector (such as the local management of water selling points) are seldom encountered but could fill an important role.

9. Often technical issues (including technical operation and maintenance) are given priority over management and contribution systems. Someone in the project team must be made responsible for facilitating the identification, development and selection of management and contribution options.

10.3.5 Responding to future demand

Projects sometimes fail because systems have not been established to meet or regulate future demand. Unmet demand can result in users reverting to traditional sources. Alternatively, various coping strategies emerge which are technically, environmentally or financially unsustainable (see Box 10.5).

Demand for water supply and sanitation is dynamic. Population change and the influence of economic and social development not only affect the types of service that people want, but also how these are valued. Unmet demand can erode the sustainability of a project and eventually cause its downfall.

Future demand has to be responded to, either by meeting it or regulating it, and this has significant implications for how projects are planned, implemented and managed.

Box 10.5. Unmet demand for yard connections

Mars is a rural settlement in Northern Province, South Africa, with a population of about 2,000 living in 315 households. Work started on a new piped water scheme in 1996, with a main pipe supplying 17 communal standpipes. At the time it was recommended that households should pay a flat rate of 5 Rand (about US$ 0.75) per month.

By May 2000, an estimated 80% of households had installed informal yard connections. Although the scheme was designed to provide a continuous supply, at the time of the visit, water was being made available for four hours a day, two to three days a week. The practice of leaving taps on and filling 200 litre drums had resulted in an unreliable service, with some households suffering from low pressure or not receiving any water at all. Average consumption was estimated between 10 and 13 litres per capita day.

The flat rate tariff had not been changed in the five years since the scheme was commissioned. With less than 60% of households paying their bills, the local water committee was reluctant to increase pumping hours even though the source had significant spare capacity.

When the project was completed, no system had been established to manage upgrading to a higher level of service, periodically review and reset both tariffs and pumping hours or deal with defaulters.

Deverill and Wedgwood (2001)

Designing for future demand presents a number of challenges to project staff, who usually have limited opportunities to interact with the scheme's future managers. It is particularly difficult to predict population growth, an 'upgrade rate', or how people's perceptions may change as their exposure to higher service levels increases. These problems are significantly reduced if a number of practical measures are used:

General

- Know the limitations of the resources available (in particular, this applies to the safe yield of a water source and the ability to dispose of waste water).

- If water is likely to be scarce, promote water-saving technologies, practices and water conservation from the beginning of a project, rather than leaving this to a management committee to sort out at a later stage.

- Ensure that current demand is met as far as possible.

- Estimate future demand for higher service levels, based on dialogue with potential users and demand assessment techniques. Consult with the authorities responsible for planning developments and allocating land.

- Reflect the need to manage future demand in both management and payment systems and the infrastructure provided.

Management systems

- Ensure that those responsible for the future management of a project are exposed to the potential problem of future demand and are fully involved in developing systems that can deal with this issue.

- Develop, test and practice systems to manage future demand during project preparation and implementation. These may include devising and agreeing rules, promoting water conservation, tariff changes, and systems for upgrading and extending a service.

- Be prepared for the unexpected. It is often difficult to predict what will happen. In Tanzania, the population of some villages doubled after a water supply was installed. Potential problems should be identified and discussed.

- If external technical, managerial or financial support is likely to be needed, establish and, if possible, practise those linkages during project preparation and implementation.

Infrastructure

- Model the impact of future demand scenarios on the proposed design. A spreadsheet can be used to help determine the sensitivity of a design to changes in consumption.

- Adopt a modular design with spare capacity or upgrade potential, based on estimates of future demand. For example, gravity flow schemes can be designed for open flow, with storage being introduced at a later stage. Another example featuring a modular design is described in Box 10.6. and Figure 10.10.

- Make maximum use of upgradable levels of service and replicable technologies. A diagram showing how a household latrine could be upgraded is shown in Figure 10.11.

- Ensure that those responsible for upgrading and extension have the training, tools and if possible the experience they require to undertake this role before a project enters its operation phase.

EZINQENI - MPINI WATER SUPPLY

— Built during implementation

········· Built after implementation

(2)

120mm riser main designed for 50l pcd for combined population of Ezinqeni, Mpini and uThungwini. Project rules state no connections to be made directly into rising main.

(1)

Manifold, pump house and pump control panel designed to accommodate second pump.

Lake Sibhayi

(5)

Private yard tap connected to nearest 5 kl tank, not to distribution pipe. Trickle feed option could be offered.

(3)

Two 50 kl ferrocement tanks built by community under supervision. Provision for third tank to extend system to uThungwini when funding becomes available.

(4)

Distributed storage system based on a total of 23 x 5 kl ferrocement tanks built by community teams. Each connected to 1 or 2 communal taps, upgradable to 12 private connections at 50l pcd). If necessary, network can be extended by building more tanks and fitting more communal taps.

(6)

School connection for drinking water only, supplemented by 2 x 5 kl roof tanks for hand washing and cleaning latrines.

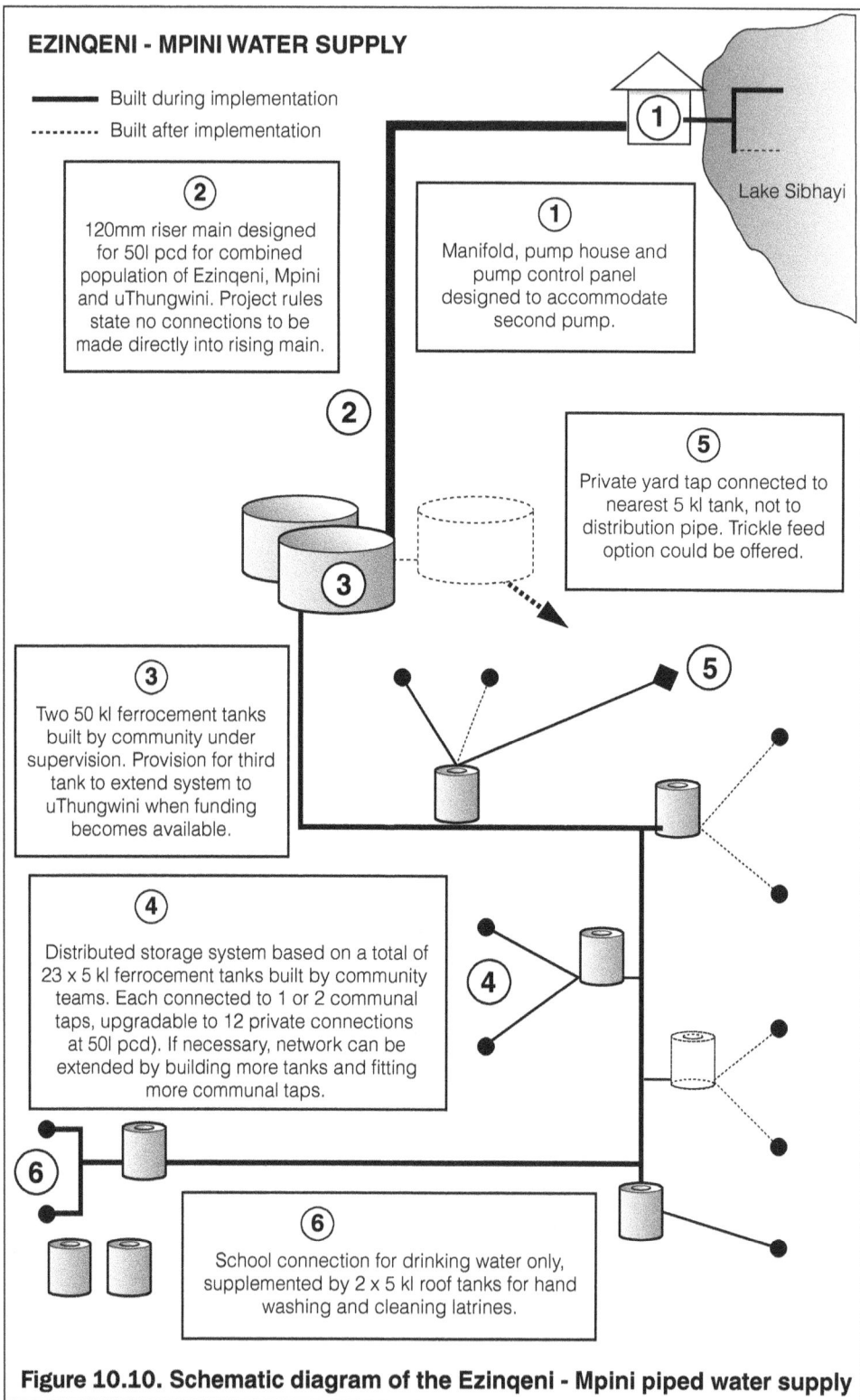

Figure 10.10. Schematic diagram of the Ezinqeni - Mpini piped water supply

Box 10.6. Ezinqeni-Mpini Water Supply

Figure 10.10 is a schematic diagram based on part of the Ezinqeni-Mpini piped water supply in KwaZulu Natal, South Africa. The scheme was designed and implemented by Partners in Development, and illustrates many of the technical features described in this Section.

The scheme was designed in 1996 for the Ezinqeni and Mpini communities, consisting of about 200 Zulu households with a characteristically dispersed settlement pattern. It was intended that at some point the piped network would be extended to uThungwini, a neighbouring community of 100 households. The extension was completed in 1999 by a second implementing organisation.

The piped water system consisted of:

- A pump manifold fitted with one pump (with provision for one more)

- A pump control panel (with the capacity to control two pumps operating in parallel)

- A riser main sized to meet an average water demand of 50 lpcd for the predicted population of Ezinqeni, Mpini and uThungwini in 10 years time.

- Two 50 kl ferrocement tanks for Ezinqueni and Mpini. The pipework was designed to supply a third for uThungwini.

- Distributed storage provided by 23 5kl ferrocement tanks located on high ground in Ezinqeni and Mpini, gravity fed from the larger tanks. The distribution pipes were sized to accommodate continuous rather than peak flow. Costs savings were used to build the 5 kl tanks.

- 25 communal taps (this number was increased to about 40), with scope for up to 12 private connections to each 5 kl tank.

Although the technical design proved highly effective, in retrospect, management and contribution systems capable of responding to future demand did not receive sufficient emphasis. A savings fund to help households pay for private connections may have proved useful. Such a scheme would need to be established in the early stages of implementation.

Deverill and Wedgwood (2001)

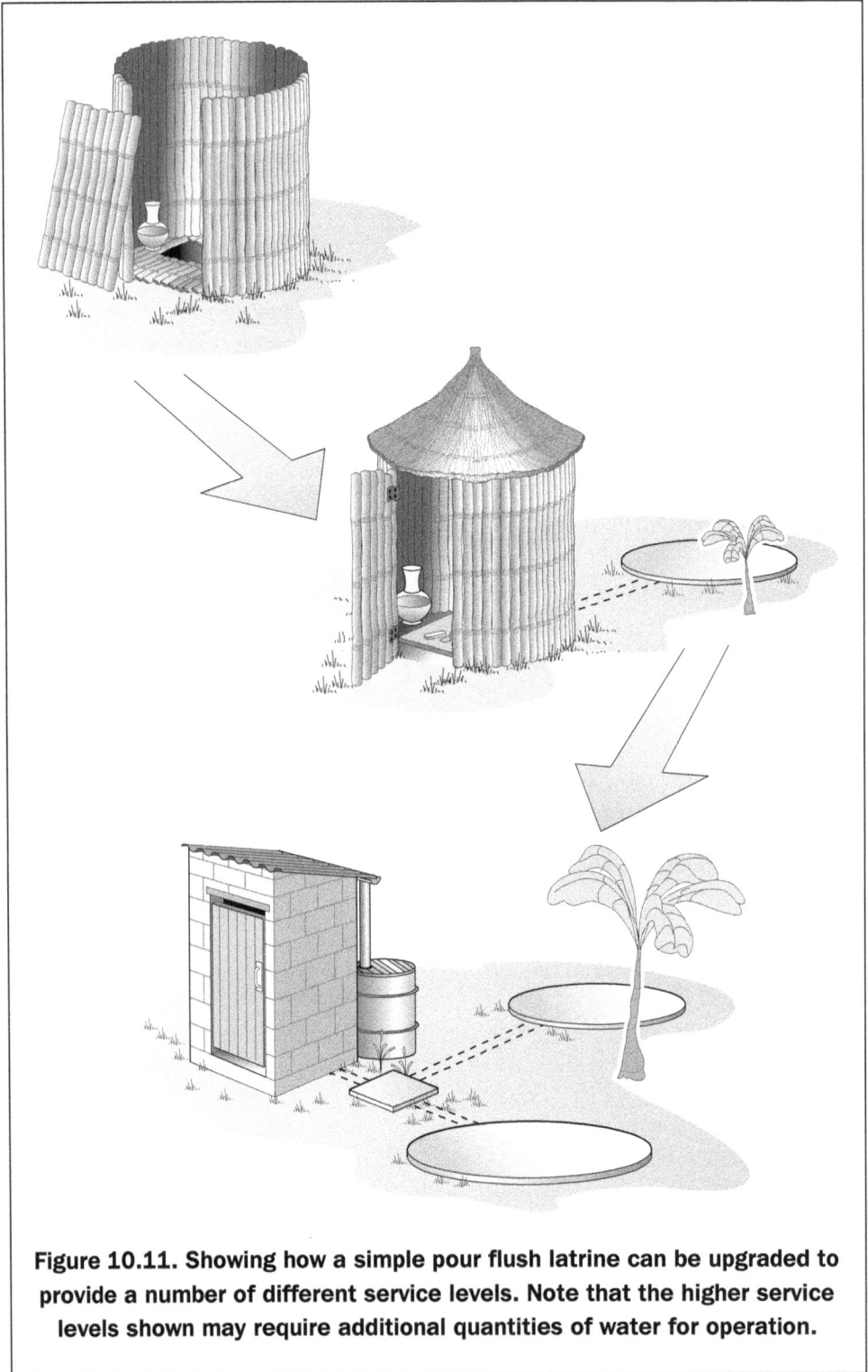

Figure 10.11. Showing how a simple pour flush latrine can be upgraded to provide a number of different service levels. Note that the higher service levels shown may require additional quantities of water for operation.

10.4 Costing, pricing and subsidies

The price of an option should be based on two factors: the actual cost of delivering the service (and of sustaining it) and people's willingness to pay for it. In practice, prices are sometimes fixed in an ad-hoc manner that does not take into account either of these factors.

The need for subsidies for the poor will continue. However, these need to be carefully designed and well-targeted, taking into account user demand. A poorly designed subsidy policy may not only be financially unsustainable, but can create a sense of dependency, with users treated as passive beneficiaries with little or no role in decision-making.

Costing options: what to include?

When costing an option, it is important to know what to include in the calculations. A number of different measures can be used, and these are listed below. It may be possible to link different measures with particular service levels, although this can be difficult to manage and higher charges for some may in any case be passed on to the poor by vendors or private sales.

Some of the more common ways of costing services include:

- Routine operation and maintenance (O&M), excluding major repairs.

- Full O&M costs.

- Full O&M plus a proportion (%) of capital costs (those costs associated with the initial provision of infrastructure).

- Full O&M, % capital and a proportion of replacement costs.

- Full O&M, capital and replacement costs.

- Full economic costing, taking into account any environmental and social costs (for example, incurred by down stream users being deprived of a water source) and the cost of expanding the system in the future. Whilst it is unlikely that users would be able to pay for the full economic costs, it is a good method of comparing different proposals.

Several of these measures are shown schematically in the following graph. As this implies, it may be possible to move from one cost measure to another in a series of incremental steps, gradually reducing the dependency on external subsidies. Such a policy could be associated with upgrading service levels.

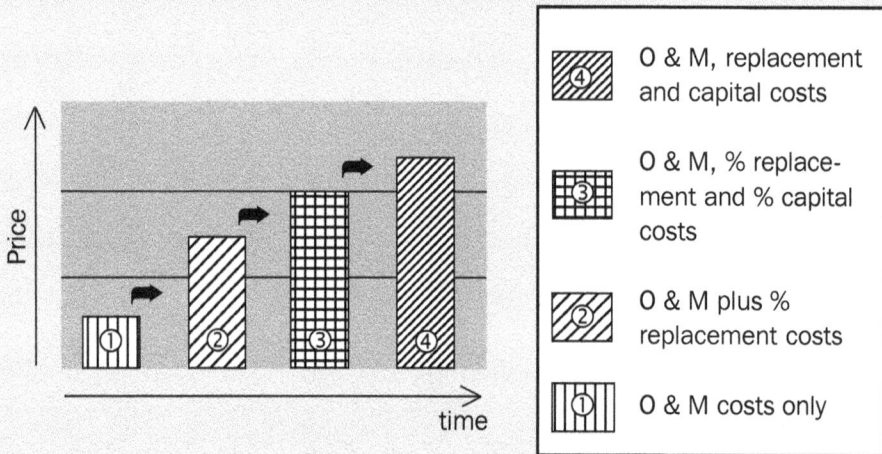

The long-term goal may be to reach full economic pricing where users pay for the full environmental and social cost of expanding the system. In practice, achieving even moderate levels of cost recovery will be a major step forward for many projects.

One strategy, adopted by several implementing organisations, is to charge full O&M costs to users receiving a basic service. People wanting higher levels of service pay all the additional capital costs associated with that option. They also pay O&M charges (like everyone else) and a proportion of the scheme's capital and replacement costs. This system may be reflected in a pricing structure that takes into account the volume of water people consume.

If such a pricing structure is used, care must be taken that it does not penalise the poor because the higher rates associated with higher levels of service (or higher consumption) are simply passed on to them. For example, several poor families may be renting rooms in a single building fitted with a private connection. People who buy water from vendors or neighbours (who have to pay tariffs reflecting their consumption) may also be disadvantaged in the same way.

Pricing, cost recovery and tariff design are subjects covered by a set of guidelines being written and produced by Environmental Resources Management (ERM). For further details, see ERM (2002).

Our research has shown that:

- Costs are not always calculated correctly, and in some cases are not calculated at all. As a result, the prices set by local management organisations may be insufficient to sustain a project.

- Replacement costs are seldom taken into account, resulting in problems when infrastructure requires renewal.

- Different service levels have different costs. This is not always reflected in the prices charged, something that often discriminates against the poor who end up paying relatively more per unit of water consumed.

- Pricing rarely takes into account people's demand for an option, and in particular their willingness to pay for a particular service or service level.

- Subsidies are often badly targeted and rarely benefit the poorest households who may need them.

The remainder of this section looks at costing options, establishing willingness to pay, setting prices and allocating subsidies in more detail.

10.4.1 Costing options

Establishing the cost of a service or facility is as important as getting the technical design right. The following points should be borne in mind:

- Information about the reliability of infrastructure and its associated cost is often difficult to obtain. It is important to start investigating this issue whilst conducting a technical review during the preparation of a project strategy.

- Costs are not just financial but often involve other requirements (inputs). For example, the following inputs may be associated with a household latrine:
  - Land on which to place it.
  - Regular cleaning, for which time and water may be required.
  - Soap and water for hand washing; water, paper or other materials for anal cleansing.
  - Regular maintenance and periodic emptying.

- Many costs are location specific, taking into account the need to find, purchase and collect materials or spares.

- Replacement costs are often omitted in calculations, possibly because they are incurred outside the project's immediate time 'horizon'. However, in some cases, major components need replacing after only a few years use due to accident, theft or normal wear and tear.

- To ensure transparency and accountability, people should know how costs are calculated.

- The cost of delivering and sustaining an option will often depend on its popularity, due to the influence of economies of scale. This reinforces the need to set prices after conducting some form of demand assessment to confirm people's willingness to pay.

Example 1: Costing a piped water supply

An example showing a breakdown of possible O&M and replacement costs (in US $) for a pumped water supply is shown in Table 10.2. The data is based on the costs of an existing scheme in KwaZulu Natal serving about 200 households.

Cost area	Monthly cost $	Source of information
Table 10.2. Operating and replacement cost analysis for a community piped water supply		
Fuel costs [ii]	$ 180	Based on an 8 hour pumping day
Motor and pump servicing costs[ii]	$ 20	Based on local experience, taking into account spares and technical expertise
Motor and pump replacement fund [iii]	$ 16	In this case, based on an 10 year lifespan and an interest rate of 15% (for details see below)
Pipe network spares	$ 15	Local experience of neighbouring schemes
Pump operator's salary	$ 40	Part time skilled wage
Caretaker's salary	$ 40	Part time skilled wage
Book keeper's salary	$ 30	Part time skilled wage
Administration	$ 25	Local experience
Sub-total	$ 366	Assumed 100% cost recovery
Additional increment	$ 92	Based on 25% non-payment rate
Total	**$ 458**	

Notes

(i)   These figures are based on supplying 20 litres per capita day. This equates to an 8 hour pumping day or 240 pumping hours per month.

(ii)   The servicing schedule and related costs are calculated from the anticipated operating hours and the manufacturer's handbook.

(iii) There are many ways of calculating capital replacement costs, some of which compensate for the time value of money.

<u>The time value of money</u>

The value of money is related to inflation and interest rates in the local and international economy. The value of $1 today will purchase more goods than $1 in five years time. Therefore, communities and project staff should be encouraged to think about how prices of local and imported components might change over their life-time to ensure that O&M replacement costs can be paid for in the future.

If users do not save for the replacement of major components, the sustainability of most water supply and sanitation projects may be short lived.

One way to do this is to set aside an equal amount (or annuity) every year, taking into account the local interest rate[19]. This is known as *amortization*, and is based on an annuity factor (AF) which can be calculated from financial cost tables. Its value is a function of the expected life-span of the component in years (n) and the interest rate (r) in the national economy.

$$\text{Annuity} = \frac{\text{Current replacement cost}}{\text{Annuity factor } (AF_{n,r})}$$

Annuity factors are tabulated in Annex A at the end of this book. The formula for calculating annuity factors is fairly complicated. As long as implementers understand that the annual amount saved should be slightly higher than the current price of a component divided by its expected lifespan in years, the community will be in a better position to replace the part concerned.

Example 2: Costing a handpump

Estimating the cost of a handpump can be relatively simple. The following example is based on the Finnish Nira hand pump, used in many countries including Tanzania, from where the following data originates[20].

In 2000, the local cost of a Nira handpump in Tanzania was about 625 US $ (for a shallow well about 8 metres deep. O&M costs are set out in the Table 10.3, and average 56 US $ per year.

---

[19] In practice interest rates are often linked to inflation.

[20] For further details see Concern Worldwide (2000).

Item	Unit cost (US $)	Annual cost (US $)
Sleeve bearing, required every 2 years	33	17
Standing plate, required every 5 years	65	13
Cylinder pipe, every 3-5 years	20	5
Six M12 nuts and washers every year	1	6
Wages for pump attendant	NA	15
TOTAL		56 US $

Table 10.3. Estimated O&M costs of the Nira AF 85 handpump

In this case, if the pump is well maintained, after 10 years its life can be extended by a further 10 years by replacing a number of critical components. These have a current price of $ 314.

The amount that needs to be set aside each year to raise enough funds to purchase these components in 10 years time can be calculated using an annuity factor. Once again, the appropriate annuity factor can be looked up in Annex A and used to calculate In this case, assuming an interest rate of 5%;

$AF_{(10,5)} = 7.72$

Annuity = 314/7.72 = $ 40.6 per year

Finally, replacement costs for the hand-pump valued at $625 can calculated, based on a 20 year life span. Again, applying an annuity factor to the present value of the hand pump ($ 625) results in an annual cost of $ 50.2

$AF_{(20,5)} = 12.46$

Annuity = 625/12.46 = $ 50.2 per year

The resulting costs of the Nira handpump are summarised in the following table.

Table 10.4. Summary of O&M and replacement costs for the Nira handpump	
Cost Description	**Annual cost (US $)**
O&M costs (recurrent)	56.0 $
10 year refit	40.6 $
20 year replacement	50.2 $
Total annual costs, years 1-10	146.8
Total annual costs, years 11-20	106.2

Table 10.4 shows that in order to enjoy the benefits of the handpump in the future, its users should set aside almost 150 $ a year for the first ten years. Assuming the pump is used by 30 families and a flat rate payment system, this is equivalent to 5 $ per household per year. This figure does not include the costs of tool replacement, every day caretaking and the cost recovery system itself. For a point water source in a small village, this last component can be very high unless a flat rate or equitable share system[21] is used.

In many communities, what happens in practice is that people wait until the handpump breaks down. At that stage, the community - or better-off households within it, may club together to pay for a repair. This could be termed *reactive* cost recovery.

When presenting costs to users, it is recommended that the advantages and disadvantages of planned and reactive cost recovery are discussed. The characteristics of each system are compared in Table 10.5

---

[21] Flat rate household payments can be made more equitable by taking into account three factors - the distance to the source, the number of people in the household, and 'special' factors such as disability. The proportion of the cost paid by each household can be agreed by the users themselves using a simple matrix.

Table 10.5. Comparison of reactive and planned cost recovery

Reactive cost recovery	Planned cost recovery
Low regular charges - or no charges at all.	Charges may be significantly higher (for example, see Table 10.4).
No major fund to look after - reduced need for management systems and accountability	Requirement to manage accumulating funds - increased need for financial management skills and accountability.
Breakdowns may be very expensive to repair compared to costs of preventative maintenance, and may occur at time when financial resources are scarce.	Opportunities to use funds for development - e.g. to start a rolling fund for sanitation improvements or small-scale production. However, this requires management skills.
Breakdowns may take time to fix - if they are fixed at all.	Regular payments may be required for a number of maintenance options, for example, a leasing arrangement.
Payment for repairs may take into account local perceptions of poverty.	Problems may arise if a breakdown occurs well before it is anticipated.

10.4.2 Testing demand for developed options

Once they have been developed and costed, options can be tested to establish people's demand, including their willingness to pay for them. This process is referred to as demand assessment, although this term can also be used to describe the measurement of demand in any stage during the project process (for example, see Section 8.2). In general, the less that users have participated in the identification and development of options, the greater will be the need for thorough demand assessment at this stage.

Assessing demand for developed options can be used to:

■ Establish what people are willing to pay to receive and sustain particular options. This information can be used to design a pricing or tariff structure.

■ Predict future demand for higher service levels, in other words, the upgrading rate.

■ Establish whether any particular group risks being disadvantaged or excluded.

■ Assess the degree of confidence that members of the public have in the development process itself and the key stakeholders involved.

Various techniques have been developed to assess demand in this way. In all cases, each option is described in detail before asking those involved to state what they would be willing to pay to receive it. The validity of the response depends on (or is contingent on) users receiving the option as it has been described. For this reason, the techniques used can be considered as different forms of contingent valuation[22].

There are two main types of contingent valuation, based on whether people are involved individually, as in the case of a one-to-one interview that forms part of a larger survey, or collectively, as in a focus group discussion. In

---

[22] Contingent valuation has already been mentioned in Section 8.2.2 That concerns its use as a tool to predict likely demand so that it can be reflected in a project strategy. In this section, the same technique is being used to confirm demand for developed options later on in a project.

practice, the term contingent valuation methodology (CVM) is formally used to describe the first type of exercise. The basic characteristics of discussion based and interview based techniques are compared in Table 10.6.

The most important distinction is that CVM can produce statistically useable data which can then be analysed to identify or rule out bias. This requires a statistics package or spreadsheet - and an experienced analyst. By comparison, group based techniques are more subjective, but allow people to discuss issues with their peers before making up their mind. Discussions need careful facilitation to avoid them being dominated by an elite.

An example demonstrating the use of CVM is described in Box 10.7. This concerns assessing demand for improved water supplies in informal street settlements in Dar es Salaam. A key objective of the exercise was to establish how much users would be willing to pay to receive an improved service. Details of how to implement a simplified form of CVM in peri-urban areas and informal settlements are found in Wedgwood and Sansom (2001).

Table 10.6. Comparison of demand assessment techniques

Discussion based demand assessment	Interview based demand assessment (CVM)
Description Facilitated focus groups are presented with a menu of options, including details of potential costs and benefits. Options are usually presented in the form of a sanitation or water ladder (see Figure 10.8) Participants discuss the relative merits of each option, before signalling how much they are prepared to contribute to receive or sustain it. People can be given a range of prices to choose from to help them make this choice.	**Description** Selected householders are interviewed by an enumerator as part of a survey. Enumerator describes options to the respondent, before asking how much the person would be willing to pay. Respondents are asked to state how much they would be willing to pay, by responding to a series of price options. Bias is managed by varying the order in which price questions are given. Once information is collected, data are processed to establish relationship between price and popularity.
Requirements Trained facilitators are required to ensure process is not dominated by an elite and that focus is retained.	**Requirements** Enumerators require training. Questionnaires must be carefully designed and tested. Statistics software or spreadsheet required for data processing.
Factors to Consider Engineers can enter dialogue with potential users. Numbers consulted are necessarily limited. Results may not reflect views of population as a whole. Participants may not give accurate answers due to influence of group. Time and experienced facilitation is needed to ensure process captures people's perceptions.	**Factors to Consider** Numbers involved are limited by resources available. Minimum number of respondents needed to achieve statistically valid result. Reliance on interviews may result in respondent not understanding the questions being asked. Dependency on specialist expertise and minimum size of survey can make CVM prohibitively expensive.

WaterAid (Dar es Salaam) is in the process of developing a simpler form of demand assessment, combining the interview technique with group discussions. Similar techniques have been tried elsewhere. One of these, known by its acronym PREPP, has recently been developed by WEDC for use in high-density informal settlements. This technique is described in Box 10.8.

Box 10.7. The use of CVM in Dar es Salaam

WaterAid Tanzania recently used CVM to investigate demand for water supply and sanitation improvements in a number of street settlements in the Temeke municipality of Dar es Salaam. The process was facilitated by an external consultant over three weeks including data processing.

A questionnaire was first developed, based on an assessment of people's coping strategies and a number of service level options. A local artist was used to represent options on a number of cards. Enumerators were selected from local government, NGOs and the communities themselves, receiving training before testing the questionnaire on a number of households.

In total, 420 households were interviewed. About half the respondents were women, 15% of which headed households. The results were then processed in the UK using a spreadsheet.

Despite the outwardly similar appearance of people's houses, the survey revealed the extent that their preferences differed. Demand could only be met by providing mixed service levels.

The survey confirmed that a significant proportion of households were willing to pay up to US $100 to receive a private connection. In the past, WaterAid had focused on communal water points.

Lessons Learnt

1. The selection and training of enumerators is very important. In this case, the involvement of local people was very useful as they were able to establish a rapport with respondents.

2. More emphasis was needed to establish the costs of different options. It was particularly difficult to cost extensions of the government piped water supply.

3. Options must be environmentally feasible. WaterAid may not be willing to offer higher levels of service to all that demand them because this may exceed the safe yield of the boreholes involved.

4. Although the quality of the CVM is important, so too is the willingness of the client to use the results to inform policies and plans.

Ndezi and Wedgwood (2001)

Box 10.8. The PREPP approach

PREPP (Participation, Ranking, Experience, Perceptions and Partnership) has been developed and tested in high-density informal settlements. It involves a facilitator, focus group and an engineer, and is relatively rapid, taking a few hours to work through its five steps.

Steps

1. A water ladder, consisting of a range of pre-tested pictures, is used to examine people's experience of existing water sources.

2. Participants are asked to rank their preferences by placing markers against each relevant picture, explaining their choice.

3. The group discusses their perceptions of the water utility and the service it provides.

4. Participants are presented with pictures representing future options, complete with estimated costs, together with the most popular existing sources. Individual preferences are indicated.

5. Finally, household expenditure charts are used to confirm how people allocate financial resources.

The value of PREPP is that it facilitates dialogue between potential users and engineers, helping ensure that people's experience and preferences are reflected in the service and facilities provided.

Sansom et al (2000)

10.4.3 Pricing

The results of a demand assessment exercise should be used to set prices that reflect demand for different options. The following associated points are particularly important:

1. Willingness to pay
Prices should be informed by the results of demand assessment. Some of the techniques that can be used in this context have been described in the preceding section.

2. Adjusting prices
Prices may need to be periodically adjusted. The organisation responsible for cost recovery must be able and sufficiently confident to do this.

3. Transparency and accountability
The pricing process must be transparent and accountable. The mechanism used to set, review and adjust prices should be approved by users. Some sort of regular audit may be required to ensure that public confidence is maintained.

4. Pro-poor strategies
The effect of a pricing strategy on poor users must be checked before it is implemented. What at first may seem a pro-poor policy may turn out to have a negative impact. For example, a rising block tariff may result in poor families which share a single tap in a rented block paying the highest tariff rate.

5. Appropriate payments
Although a service can be priced in non-monetary terms, for example, requiring a payment of rice or corn, this serves no purpose if the product used cannot be converted into the inputs needed to receive or sustain the service.

6. Emergency funds
Some implementing organisations require that users contribute towards an emergency fund. This results in a relatively large sum of money being deposited in a savings account. Even though interest is being paid, users may feel that this is not using their contribution effectively and that the system lacks accountability. It may be possible to mobilise a proportion of these funds for other purposes, for example, to start a revolving fund.

10.4.4 Subsidies

Given the limited resources available to some households it is inevitable that subsidies will continue to be needed. However, they need to be well targeted. In practice, subsidies are often claimed by better-off households and seldom reach those most in need (WELL (1998) p108).

The requirement for subsidies can be reduced by developing low cost options, and improving access to credit or payment by instalment. A low cost option however will only be a satisfactory solution to the extent that it meets people's demands – if it is perceived as inferior they may not be willing to pay for it or maintain it. In addition, savings and credit facilities tend to be used by the better off rather than the poor, many of whom are in debt.

In some cases, a relatively small, well-targeted subsidy can have a significant impact, both by making a basic option more affordable and also by motivating people to take action. UNICEF and other organisations have learnt the following lessons:

■ Always find out what people are willing to contribute before designing a subsidy programme.

■ Investigate and, if possible, build on local practices concerning cross-subsidies.

■ Investigate opportunities for local cross subsidies. For example, commercial users who profit from their use of water could be charged a higher rate. However, it is important to ensure that this does not impact negatively on the poor, for example if higher rates are simply passed on.

■ If policies permit, household subsidies can be managed locally and allocated according to local perceptions of need (for example, see Box 10.9). The result can be more efficient targeting and a greater overall impact.

■ Consider providing subsidies in the form of materials or specialist advice rather than cash.

■ Establish systems that can account for how subsidies are used.

■ Only subsidise a basic level of service, with the additional costs of higher service levels being borne by the users themselves.

■ Ensure that the subsidised price of options still reflects the level of service being provided.

■ Never give subsidies as a short-term fix to increase coverage.

■ Be transparent in developing and implementing a subsidy policy.

Adapted from EHP (1997) and others

The following example illustrates how NEWAH has used wealth ranking to target subsidies more effectively in rural communities in Nepal.

Box 10.9. Using wealth ranking to target subsidies

NEWAH has a policy of continuously refining its policies. The creation of a Poverty and Gender group has helped focus attention on these particular issues. One tangible result has been the recent introduction of a wealth ranking exercise, the results of which are used to target subsidies more effectively.

A group of 10-13 people are selected by the community to participate in the exercise and identify suitable indicators. Typical criteria are shown in the box below (left). Every household is then placed in one of six socio-economic groups. The characteristics of group 5 are shown in the box (right). The lowest group (group 6) includes the landless poor who have to work in other people's fields to survive.

Criteria for Wealth Ranking	**Example: group 5 characteristics**
■ Land ownership ■ Business ownership ■ Employment ■ Indebtedness and "bandha" or bonded labours ■ Type of home ■ Food security	■ Home owner ■ Own small parcel of land ■ Large family size ■ Loan taken ■ Some family members "bandha"

The results of the exercise are then used to determine who contributes what. This applies to the initial cash contribution as well as regular O&M payments. Sanitation slabs are provided free to those in groups 5 and 6. Those in groups 4, 5 and 6 are favoured when it comes to employment. Vulnerable households are not expected to contribute voluntary labour, but get a basic wage.

Bajracharya and Deverill (2001)

PREP ➤ SEL ➤ PLAN ➤ APP ➤ IMP ➤ OP ➤

Appraising a community plan

In the last section we have seen how a menu of options can be identified, developed and costed. Demand can then be assessed using an appropriate technique. The results of the demand assessment may then be used to help set prices and to gauge the popularity of individual options.

The resulting information can be put together in the form of a planning report that includes a detailed design (including a menu of options), a budget and a schedule of activities and tasks.

One purpose of such a document could be to inform the project's funder (whether this be government, an international donor or an intermediary) about the outcomes of the planning process, and in particular:

- The alternatives considered.
- The decisions which were taken.
- The process by which decisions were made.
- The options to be presented.

It is also possible to present the plan to the community for their formal approval. The form this takes and the methods used must be tailored to suit the needs of the audience.

In the UNICEF supported water supply and sanitation projects in Orissa, community action plans are represented on a large exterior wall in the centre of each village concerned. This dramatic visual aid provides a focus and a reference point for the discussions that follow. The plan continues to be used as a backdrop for subsequent meetings and open discussions, and eventually becomes a monitoring tool against which progress is checked.

If a local organisation (this could be a watsan committee, a government department, an NGO or a private company) is to be responsible for implementing the project, it should be prepared to present and discuss it in this way, answering questions and responding to people's concerns.

Such a presentation should include details of what the options are, the contributions needed to receive and sustain them, and how they are to be made available. It should also include a realistic time frame.

The final stage of such a meeting could involve a vote of approval for both the plan and the local management organisation that will be involved in its execution. This in itself is an indicator of demand. Approval could also be supported by a decision to start collecting the contribution required.

Unicef WES (Orissa)

A community map used to present an action plan in a village in Ganjam District, Orissa

This underlines the point that users who take key decisions on behalf of others have responsibilities both to the project's funder and the households they represent. The role of project staff changes from implementing a project on behalf of passive beneficiaries to (i) facilitating users to make informed decisions about the services they require and (ii) providing advice to a local management organisation that is responsible for executing a community plan.

PREP ──▶ SEL ──▶ PLAN ──▶ APP ──▶ IMP ──▶ OP ⟹

11. Implementing a community plan

Implementation is not just about construction. Firstly, users have to choose which option they want to receive. The result may be mixed levels of service. It is likely that not every user will get his or her first choice and that some sort of negotiated compromise will be required.

Implementation is also the stage in the project when concrete demonstrations of demand can be used most effectively to guide project progress. Appropriate indicators of demand have to be selected which are clearly linked with the service and service levels being provided.

Finally, implementation provides the opportunity for project staff to formalise technical, contribution and management systems. These will underpin the longer-term sustainability of the services being provided.

Decision-making and financial control

Decision-making and financial control are inevitably linked. Most key decisions have financial implications. If decisions are to be made by users or their representatives, key aspects of financial control should be devolved as well.

Project staff may want to devolve decision-making, but can be reluctant to let users make decisions which have important financial implications. This is hardly surprising, as an implementing organisation has responsibilities to the project's funder, and often has to bear the risk of failure.

Organisations like Mvula Trust believe that communities must take financial control, but this must be founded on effective capacity building and training to ensure that funds are well managed. The system is supported by safeguards and monitoring, although this results in additional bureaucracy and occasional time delays.

11.1 Presenting and agreeing options

The key to presenting and agreeing service options is an effective communication strategy. This could inform users of the following:

- How the project is going to be implemented, including details of its management structure, budget, time-frame, reporting and feedback arrangements.

- Which service level options are available. This should include a detailed description of their characteristics, including their upgradability. It is also important to detail any constraints that may narrow choice in certain areas or situations.

- The type and size of contribution required to receive and to sustain each service level option. There may be a choice of contribution methods. If costs are sensitive to the popularity of an option, this should also be explained, with a price range being supplied instead.

- How the prices charged are related to the costs of providing and sustaining the service.

- Details of any local rules or by-laws that apply. For example, it is important that a user of a piped water supply understands the implications of not paying before he or she opts for that system.

- Finally, how users can apply to receive a particular service level and how long this process is expected to take.

- The communication techniques referred to in Section 10.3.2 can be used or adapted to get these messages across.

It may be appropriate for users to demonstrate their preferences by applying for a particular level of service. The application process should be carefully managed, especially if a cash deposit is concerned, in which case transparency and accountability are particularly important. Practically, it may be necessary to cluster households in order that the service can be delivered as efficiently as possible.

One of the key responsibilities for project staff is to try to meet user preferences as far as is technically and economically practicable. It is likely that not everyone is going to be satisfied. For example, it may prove impossible to supply a family tube well because the water table is too deep in that particular location. This situation is better handled if:

- Users understand from an early stage that it may not be possible to meet their first preference.

- Demand for options has already been properly assessed, giving project staff and local managers a good indicator of what to expect.

- A number of alternative options exist.

- Local investigations are conducted (and if necessary deposits returned) quickly.

- Project staff and local management are seen to be concerned and do their best to resolve the situation.

A flexible, common-sense attitude is often required. For example, if the majority of households opt for yard taps, whilst a small minority of poor households opt for communal wells, it may be possible to arrange a local cross subsidy and provide a piped system with yard taps and communal stand pipes instead of communal wells.

11.2 Using demonstrations of demand

Before the implementation stage of the project, there have been relatively few opportunities for all users to demonstrate their demand for improved services. It is possible that people did contribute a deposit or 'feasibility fee' during the selection process. Representative groups of users (for example, those in focus groups) and appointed managers may have been heavily involved during the planning phase.

Only after options have been developed, however, is it possible to confirm household demand for a specific service and service levels.

The main reason why demonstrations of demand are needed is to indicate to project staff whether the planned service improvements do indeed match user demand. If not, there is still time for the implementing organisation to do something about it.

A range of indicators can be used as demonstrations of demand, the most important of which are described below. These must be clearly linked with the service or service levels being provided. At the same time, indicators must be carefully selected, ensuring in particular that the perceptions of vulnerable groups are represented.

Whilst the use of a range of indicators may give a more reliable picture than relying on one, project staff should not create the impression that users have to pass an endless series of demand responsive 'tests' to keep the project going.

11.2.1 Contracts

An agreed contract between the local organisation providing the service and the household receiving it can - in some circumstances - be used as an indicator of demand. Such agreements should detail both the rights and responsibilities of the parties involved. For households, the latter may include the acceptance of rules concerning the use of and payment for the services provided.

The use of contracts depends above all on their perceived authority and cultural acceptability. In practice, it may be most effective to adopt or adapt a local method of formalising an agreement. If written contracts are used, illiteracy may exclude many users, particularly women and the poor.

Ensuring the local management committee has some form of legal standing can provide a contract with additional authority. A less formal alternative could be to establish a user group or association, complete with membership cards and rules.

11.2.2 Upfront cash payments

An upfront or advanced cash payment is often considered to be a clear indicator of demand and can be important for confirming the ownership of the facilities being provided. Upfront cash contributions can also indicate a community's ability to organise and collect payments. The size of the contribution should be linked to the cost of the service being provided and an assessment of people's willingness to pay (see Section 10.4.2).

However, as an indicator of household demand, cash payments have some limitations. In some communities, a wealthy individual may put up the entire payment required. An unscrupulous contractor may do the same to secure a lucrative contract. Households with less influence may be coerced by others into making a payment, even if this means taking out an expensive loan.

The size and timing of contribution also requires careful consideration. Both factors should reflect the degree of confidence people have in the project and the realization of its outputs. This implies that contributions should be staggered during implementation.

Caution is therefore required. If an upfront cash payment is required, users should be warned well in advance in order that they can save up funds if necessary. As previously mentioned, it may be necessary for the project to establish a savings scheme. In any case, the timing of any substantial cash payment should coincide with the seasonal availability of funds. An example illustrating the use and importance of cash payments is described in Box 11.1.

Box 11.1. The significance of cash contributions

WaterAid's rural water supply and sanitation programme in Niassa Province, Mozambique, reinforces the link between cash contributions and ownership.

A key aspect of the Government's new water policy is that communities need to demonstrate their capacity to sustain a water system. One way of doing this is to make an up-front cash contribution towards the capital cost of the supply.

- The cash contribution demonstrates whether communities have the organisational and financial capacity to raise *cash*.

- It can indicate the degree of confidence users have in the project's implementers (including a local management organisation).

- It also provides some evidence of a community's interest and commitment in the scheme, as would a contribution of labour or resources.

It is however questionable whether the cash collected is an indicator of a community's ability to pay for operation and maintenance over time.

An interesting issue to emerge from the programme in Niassa is the desire of participating communities to pay for their new systems rather than contributing resources or labour. The previous national water policy in Mozambique stated that communities would feel a sense of ownership if they contributed labour and housed and fed construction teams. However, evidence from the field strongly suggested that *people believed that they owned a system only if they paid for it.*

Breslin (2000 a&b)

11.2.3 Work

A contribution of work is often required during the project implementation, and this can also be used to demonstrate demand. Rather than being completely voluntary, people may instead receive a reduced wage.

A number of points should be borne in mind:

- If people are to receive a reduced wage, this must be selected carefully. If this is too high, the project may be perceived as an income earning opportunity, with people valuing their wages rather than the service being provided. An alternative may be to provide meals during the construction period.

- The poor, especially those who have no land, may find it as difficult to contribute labour as to provide cash, because they are forced to work to earn a basic living.

- The availability of people's time is often seasonal, especially in rural areas. This underlines the value of developing an implementation time table that is based on a local calendar.

- Women often end up doing voluntary work, thereby increasing their daily burden.

- Local regulations (for example, concerning union membership and health and safety) may restrict the use of volunteers to construct infrastructure.

- Regardless of whether work is voluntary or not, it is still necessary to supervise quality.

- In some cases it may be possible to offer a degree of flexibility, accepting cash or another form of contribution instead of work.

11.2.4 Materials

The provision of materials is also a contribution that can be used to demonstrate demand. Because it involves people's labour, all of the points considered above also apply. The availability of materials is location dependent (and may also be seasonal) and this should be taken into account.

11.2.5 Time and interest

It can be relatively simple to monitor demand based on the interest people show in attending a well-publicised meeting during which critical issues are to be discussed. The meeting's purpose, location and timing must be carefully considered. A number of separate meetings may be needed to capture the social or cultural diversity of the community concerned. Having said that, too many meetings, especially if they are perceived as having little significance, can erode interest as quickly as the credibility of the organisation holding them.

Committee and focus group members are often expected to put a considerable number of hours into first developing and then implementing a plan. The difficulty sometimes experienced just getting to a meeting is often over-looked. Project staff need to be sensitive to these issues.

11.3 Preparing management for its future role

Being demand responsive and offering options that result in mixed levels of service make managing the completed project more complex. As has been made clear in Section 10 the need to respond to future demand adds to this challenge.

It is therefore essential that the local management organisation is fully pre-pared to undertake its role. Fortunately, there are many opportunities to ensure this happens that arise during project implementation.

Preparing management for its future role

The underlying principle is that all the responsibilities of a management organisation should be tested and practised during implementation.

Responsibilities for this important aspect of capacity building fall on the organisation implementing the project and in particular, on engineers who often have financial, technical and management skills. The remainder of this section details four activities, all associated with future demand, for which a local management organisation could be responsible. In each case, the tasks described should be practised and tested during implementation.

11.3.1 Price review and adjustment.

Periodically, costs should be reviewed and, if necessary, prices reset. The organisation responsible for this task must have the necessary skills and confidence to carry it out. It must also be able to communicate any changes in prices and explain its action to users.

11.3.2 Upgrading

Technical, financial and management systems are needed to ensure that the process of upgrading is managed. In some cases, upgrading will have to be carefully regulated so as not to exceed technical or environmental constraints. The provision of mixed levels of service during implementation provides opportunities for local managers and their staff to develop, test and practise the upgrading mechanism.

11.3.3 Expansion

Expansion does not simply mean extending a pipeline, but also replicating facilities such as wells or latrines to respond to unmet demand. Extending a piped water supply may require external financial and technical support. Responsibilities for providing this support should be agreed during project preparation. During implementation, any mechanism for requesting and receiving external support should be practised. External support will be more effective if it has access to as-built drawings which detail what was actually implemented (rather than what was intended).

A simple management tool that can facilitate the locally managed construction of facilities such as domestic latrines, wells and tube wells is the job card. This sets out the process to be followed and the materials and other inputs required. It also provides a system to monitor quality. Job cards are described in more detail in Box 11.2.

Box 11.2. The job card

Job cards have been used by implementing organisations in South Africa, originally to facilitate the local management of sanitation programmes. They have also been used to simplify the delivery of wells and tube wells. An example of a job card is shown on the following pages. In this case it is associated with the Mbila sanitation and hygiene project, first described in Box 10.2.

The card is initiated when a householder shows interest in acquiring a latrine. Personal details are recorded and a job number allocated. The materials required (shown on the job card) are then dispatched. The householder initials the form to confirm receipt of the materials delivered.

As work proceeds, the job card details the payments that should be made. A checklist on the reverse of the card is used to check the quality of the work before the latrine is finally handed over to the customer.

As a management tool, the job card sets out the process by which a service is delivered, simplifies logistics and financial management, and helps with quality control, monitoring and evaluation. It also enables a local management team to check on progress. It has proved particularly effective when a local management organisation was faced with the problem of responding to increasing demand for sanitation, allowing it to manage four construction teams simultaneously.

VIP Latrine Job Card & Handover Certificate

TRIBAL AUTHORITY:	*MBILA*		ISIGODI:		*uThungwini*

Part 1: General

Name of Householder:	Job Card No:	Receipt No:
Mike Mdletshe	**14**	**106**

Part 2: Material, Labour, Transport & Management Needs

Type	Unit	Quantity Needed	Unit Cost (R)	Total Cost (R)	Material Issued
					Initials
Cement	pockets	5	26	130	*ML*
Weld Mesh	metres	4.6	22	101	*ML*
Galvanised wire	kg	1	5	5	*ML*
Toilet lid		2	16	16	*ML*
Plastic liner		1	8	8	*ML*
110mm Vent Pipe	3 metres	1	60	30	*ML*
Fly Screen		1	2	2	*ML*
Manual		1	10	10	*ML*
					(Householder)

Builders, Transport and Management					Signature
Mbazwana Transport	Per Toilet		50	50	*HM*
Pit team	Man days	4	25	100	*TM*
Pit team leader	Man days	2	15	30	*TM*
Local transport	Per Toilet		25	50	*ST*
Quality Assessor	Per Toilet		15	150	*KL*
Book keeper	Per Toilet		10	10	*HL*
Office expenses	Per Toilet		40	40	*DZ*
Final Inspection	Per Toilet		10	10	*KL*
					(Recipient)

Figure 11.2. An example of a job card developed by the Mbila Sanitation and Hygiene Project in Kwa Zulu Natal. The quality control checklist and handover certificate are printed on the reverse.

Part 3: Quality Control and Handover Form

	Signature (QA)	Date	Remarks
1. Materials			
Materials on site	KL	10/05/1998	
(Tractor driver can be paid after materials for 10 toilets dropped off on site)			
2. Precasting Rings			
6 rings made and approved	KL	23/05/1998	
Slab and predestal cast and approved	KL	23/05/1998	
Location approved	KL	23/05/1998	
3. Sub-structure			
Pit excavated	KL	31/05/1998	
Rings backfilled	KL	31/05/1998	
Slab level	KL	31/05/1998	
Pedestal complete & ok	KL	31/05/1998	
(Builders, local driver and QA can be paid after 10 superstructures completed)			
4. Super-structure			
Ventilation	KL	22/06/1998	
Fly Screen	KL	22/06/1998	
Drainage	KL	22/06/1998	
Darkness	KL	22/06/1998	
5. Hygiene Visit			
(Signed by health worker)	JM	28/06/1998	
(QA can be paid after superstructure is completed and the deposit returned)			

11.3.4 Monitoring systems

Monitoring systems should also be established and initiated during implementation. These should be designed for use by local management, and focus on issues relating to sustainability. In this respect, monitoring the quality of the work undertaken is very important.

Monitoring quality

The potential users of the service being provided are potentially very effective monitors of quality, having a major stake in the outcome. To realise this potential, appropriate indicators of quality have to be identified, and tools and training provided. Project staff must be able to devolve this responsibility, monitoring the local monitoring system rather than the work itself.

A practical example of user based quality control has already been referred to in Box 11.2. In this case, the local management group checked the quality of each VIP (together with the householder) before handing it over.

It was the householder's responsibility to complete the superstructure. If this was deemed to be inadequate (in terms of its operation), an initial deposit of 100 Rand (about US $ 10) made by the householder would be used to set things right. Otherwise this deposit would be returned.

Monitoring demand

Other than the quality of work being undertaken, it is also important for the local management organisation to be able to monitor a number of other indicators, many of which are related to demand and therefore the sustainability of the service in question. These are described in more detail in the next section. It is however important to note that such systems must be developed, tested and put in place during implementation, whilst project staff are still available to provide advice.

11.3.5 Management manuals

To complement the training outlined above, it is recommended that the local management organisation is left with a practical manual detailing its tasks, how to carry them out, and who to contact should a problem arise. Such a manual could also include details of the technical and financial tasks that the management organisation is responsible for.

For some time it has been widely recommended that those implementing a project produce a detailed operation and maintenance manual, handing it over to a water committee once implementation has been completed. What is being suggested here is an extension of that idea. However, in this case, the manual would be developed and used during implementation as a training aid, in line with the principle defined earlier in this section:

....all responsibilities of a management organisation should be tested and practised during implementation.

The following table gives some indication of what could be included in such a manual for a piped water supply. Presentation is as important as content, with clear, simple to understand instructions being the key. In this respect, check-lists and flow charts can be very effective.

Table 11.1. Suggested contents for a management manual

1. As-built drawings of scheme showing pipe sizes and location.

2. Details of each major component or module.

3. Maintenance calendar and practical details of each maintenance task.

4. Technical notes on upgrading and extending the system.

5. Profit and loss sheets and instructions how to use them. For details see Section 12.3.

6. Tariff adjustment chart and instructions.

7. Details of monitoring system and instructions.

8. Contact details of support organisations and their responsibilities.

12. Operation

The final section in this booklet concerns both operation and maintenance (O&M) and monitoring and evaluation (M&E). In the past, these have been separated institutionally. O&M was the responsibility of local management and the users themselves, and M&E the responsibility of the external client or government agency.

More recently there has been a shift in thinking, associated with the principle that management functions should be devolved to the lowest appropriate level. If responsibilities for management are to be devolved, so too should M&E systems which can serve as a valuable management aid.

This section focuses on how a small number of demand related indicators could be used by local management to help sustain a water and sanitation project. It should be pointed out that whilst this internalises M&E, it also helps reinforce the links with mentoring and external support agencies.

12.1 Principles of community based M&E

Mvula Trust has developed a set of clear principles for community based M&E for rural water supply and sanitation projects. These are particularly appropriate for a demand responsive project and are listed below[23].

1. <u>Simplicity and ease of use</u>
Systems should be developed that take into account the capacity of those who will be using them. Only important indicators should be monitored. In terms of M&E tools, flow charts and checklists may be more appropriate than text.

---

[23] For further details, see Netshiswinzhe and Potter (2000).

2. Use of data
The information collected must be used to take corrective action, i.e. improving current performance or future programming. This requires simple reporting lines from the individual measuring the indicator to the individual who takes corrective action.

3. Focus on key sustainability issues
The focus should be on sustainability. However, it is important the this is not too narrow, for example, examining short-term concerns and leaving out long term issues. A balance has to be achieved.

4. External links
Whilst the aim is to allow local management to identify their own problems and solutions, external agencies can play an important role, depending on the local context:

- By providing a timely, appropriate response to address problems that cannot be solved at local level.

- By assisting with the measurement of certain indicators, for example, water quality, borehole yields and auditing accounts. These require less frequent measurement.

- By monitoring the M&E system itself. M&E tasks can be nested, with weekly, monthly, six monthly and annual checks being carried out by different organisations.

5. Involving women
The indicators used should reflect the particular interest women have in water and sanitation. Indicators of user satisfaction should not be limited to payments, for example, if financial resources are largely controlled by men.

12.2 Demand related indicators for managers

The following tables list demand related sanitation and water indicators. In practice, it is recommended that locally appropriate indicators are identified by the users themselves, together with their local management organisation.

Whatever is used must be perceived as being sufficiently important to measure to justify the associated effort and expense.

Table 12.1. Possible indicators for monitoring domestic sanitation	
Indicator	**Remarks**
Payments received	The number of payments received indicates demand for each option offered.
Waiting time	Demand may diminish if there is a long delay between payment and 'delivery'. A delay can indicate problems in administration, logistics or construction.
Number of latrines built	Though important in terms of potential impact and easy to measure, the number of latrines built is irrelevant if they are not used.
Use of facilities	Use is more difficult to measure. A *sanitary survey*[24] can be used to look for evidence of use. It is important to establish if all members of the household are using the latrine, and if not, why not.
Upgrading	Upgrading is a good indicator that (i) people are valuing sanitation more and (ii) there is a system that can respond to changes in demand.
Hand washing and use of soap	Related to the use of sanitation and its potential health impact, hygiene behaviour can also be monitored, again using evidence from a sanitary survey.

---

[24] For details of how to conduct a sanitary survey, see Howard (2002)

Table 12.2. Possible indicators for monitoring domestic water supply

Indicator	Remarks
Upfront cash contributions	As already discussed, an up-front contribution is a strong indicator of demand, and should be measured. This illustrates that M&E can be used during implementation, as long as systems are established.
Water availability	Demand is unlikely to be met if water is not available. This can be relatively simple to monitor on a daily or weekly basis, for example by measuring tap flows or hours of operation.
Quantity used	The amount of water used can also be a good indicator of demand. Low consumption may indicate that other sources are preferred. Measuring consumption can be difficult if meters are not installed.
Regular payment for services received	If users are not satisfied with the service they receive, they are unlikely to want to pay for it. Payment is simple to measure, and is a useful indicator of demand.
User satisfaction & complaints	It is important to measure user satisfaction (and dissatisfaction) that is not linked to payment. This may apply to women who seldom control the financial resources used to pay for water, but who have a 'majority interest' in domestic water and sanitation.
Upgrading	Upgrading is a good indicator that i) people are valuing water supply more and ii) there is a system that can respond to changes in demand.
Hand washing and use of soap	Related to the use of sanitation and its potential health impact, hygiene behaviour can also be monitored, again using evidence from a sanitary survey.

Each of these indicators can be linked to the results of a wealth ranking exercise. It may be useful for local management to focus on the poorest households that are most vulnerable to exclusion, ensuring that they are able to access and use improved services as designed.

12.3 Types of M&E tools

Mvula Trust has developed four categories of M&E tool which are useful for a demand responsive project. These are summarised here[25]. Each was piloted in a number of rural water and sanitation projects.

1. Flowcharts
Flowcharts provide a simple checklist of factors, arranging these into a logical sequence of cause and effect, indicator and action. They also highlight certain responses for follow-up. In practice, flowcharts have proved more popular and easy to use than questionnaires. An example is shown in Annex B.

2. Logbook
Most of the information needed to complete a flowchart can be recorded in a simple logbook and financial records. The logbook is a daily or weekly record of operational problems, the action taken, and the response time. In Mvula's experience, it is most effective when completed by whoever is 'on duty' at the time. The logbook encourages local management to establish a simple fault reporting line. An example of a log sheet is shown in Annex B.

3. Questionnaires
Questionnaires can be developed to deal with the same type of information used by the flow charts. Although they are more flexible in that issues can be qualified in more detail, they are more complex to complete.

4. Posters
Posters help communicate messages about the steps that users can take in certain situations. This can help with fault reporting or applying for a domestic latrine. Posters are also important in improving transparency. In the UNICEF supported water and sanitation programme in Ganjam, Orissa, the results of community monitoring were displayed for all to see. This took the form of a large poster next to the village map. In this case, households who had latrines but were not using them were identified by a red mark.

---

[25] See Netshiswinzhe and Potter, (2000)

12.4 Concluding points

Although it is important to be able to measure and respond to the parameters being measured, it is also useful to investigate how the situation is changing over time. The most important indicators can be presented pictorially on a chart.

The data collected by a local management organisation can be used to evaluate the long-term impact of a project. In this context, longer-term trends can be just as important as absolute values.

The M&E system is itself a sustainability indicator. If the monitoring system is not being used, there may be a problem with the management organisation itself.

Finally, it has been emphasised that the tools used and the parameters measured should be locally appropriate and if possible developed by users and the local management organisation. In practice, the use of common tools and indicators - shared between a number of schemes - would help the establishment of a simple, efficient project support system. A balance should be found.

13. Implications for engineers

13.1 Introduction

A demand responsive approach has implications for all project staff, influencing not only their individual roles and responsibilities, but also how they interact professionally. The consequences are likely to be especially significant for project engineers.

In a 'conventional' supply-led environment, engineers derive much of their authority and job satisfaction from the infrastructure they provide. Engineers are expected and indeed trained to take important technical decisions on behalf of the client or the project's donors.

Not surprisingly, some engineers feel uncertain about introducing a demand responsive approach that appears to contradict their training by giving people decision-making responsibilities[26]. As a result, engineers may feel marginalised by this process and may resist change, something that can add to the complexity of introducing and scaling up a demand responsive approach. For government engineers, any uncertainty may be compounded by two other development 'trends' - decentralisation and the switch from implementation to facilitation.

Reluctance to change is often associated with uncertainty about the future. Whilst this booklet is designed to clarify what designing to meet demand means in practice for all project staff, this final section looks specifically at the possible roles and responsibilities of project engineers.

13.2 The engineer's role

Considering the project process as a whole, engineers have a number of potential responsibilities that together define their role. These are listed below.

---

[26] In fact, many contemporary engineering design textbooks emphasise the importance of consulting people about the facilities they require and explain how this can be achieved using techniques similar to those described in Section 10 of these guidelines.

This list is indicative - actual responsibilities depend on the project's context and the capacity and resources available.

Developing a project strategy

- Assessing the enabling environment (consisting of policies, legislation and institutions) from a technical perspective. For details see Section 8.1.

- Establishing and developing links between project staff, communities and organisations responsible for providing longer term technical support.

- As part of an initial assessment of demand, investigating people's coping strategies and implied preferences. Such work is likely to be undertaken with a social facilitator.

- Investigating and developing a number of potential technical options. This may involve wider consultation including learning visits to other projects.

- Advising on the use of technical criteria to help select sub-projects.

Working with communities

(Each of the following tasks requires a mix of technical, social and communication skills, implying a team-based approach is necessary).

- Provide users with an *informed* choice of technical options (and quite possibly financial options) which are (i) likely to meet demand, (ii) effective in terms of addressing project objectives and (iii) technically, environmentally and financially feasible. People need to be aware of the implications of their choice. One implication is that options must be accurately costed. In overall terms, the process benefits from consultation with a range of potential users as described in Section 10. *Engineers have to be able to listen to and understand the opinions of potential users.*

- Negotiate services levels with the community, balancing demands (some of which may compete with others) with a variety of constraints including the capacity and resources available, the needs of the environment and the potential impact on others.

- Specifically ensure that vulnerable groups are included rather than excluded by providing appropriate options with the potential to meet their demands.

- Promote longer-term sustainability by developing local capacity and establishing mechanisms that can manage changes in demand at both household and community level.

Working with support organisations

- Develop the technical capacity (and maybe the financial and managerial capacity) of support organisations to help them undertake their responsibilities. This may include establishing procedures for mentoring, auditing and the provision of technical support.

Working with the project team

- *Learn* from other project staff to improve the effectiveness of technical inputs. Engineers have a responsibility to understand the cultural, social and economic aspects of people's lives and how this impacts on technology. Equally, they must also be aware of the techniques used by other project staff, their purpose, application, strengths and weaknesses.

- Develop the technical capacity (and quite possibly the financial and managerial capacity) of project staff to offer options and facilitate informed decision making.

- Provide project staff with sound advice on the technical and financial characteristics of a wide range of options.

This list of potential responsibilities is not exhaustive. It demonstrates that the engineer's role in a demand responsive environment is very different - but no less challenging than before. If anything, engineers have to apply their skills and judgement *in greater depth and more broadly* to ensure that people have an informed choice of options and mechanisms are established to support those choices.

The remainder of this section will look at what could be considered the central responsibility in more detail: providing users with options. This is followed by a summary of the knowledge, skills and attitudes that engineers need in order to design to meet demand.

13.3 Providing users with options

Providing users with an informed choice of options that reflect demand and the various constraints imposed by the natural and the enabling environment is arguably the most challenging process in a demand responsive project. To support it, engineers require the following:

13.3.1 Familiarity with a wide range of potential options

Engineers need to be familiar with a wide range of service, service level and service delivery options, their characteristics, limitations, costs and inherent flexibility. Three issues are particularly important:

- Potential options should be affordable[27]. For many people, *'unconventional' low-cost solutions* may be needed. This applies not only to the technology and materials used, but also to any mechanism used to supply, operate, maintain and upgrade services. *Engineers will be expected to establish the capital, recurrent and replacement cost of any options.*

- The options provided should take into account future changes in demand. This may mean providing upgradable levels of service. If water resources are limited, *water conservation measures* may also be important. These should not discriminate against the poor, who often use very limited amounts of water in any case.

- People's demands are likely to reflect their livelihoods rather than narrow 'sectoral' definitions of water supply and sanitation (see Section 3.1). Engineers may be required to investigate some options with which they are not familiar, for example, a small-scale irrigation system using wastewater from communal taps.

Based on the experience of the authors obtained whilst developing these guidelines, relatively few engineers have the necessary knowledge and experience to offer a full range of options. This has two major implications.

---

[27]As explained in Part I of this booklet, rather than assume an overall level of affordability, it is more effective to assess willingness to pay for particular options.

(i) The technical capacity of project engineers may need to be strengthened during the initial stages of a project. Opportunities must be identified and time and resources provided. To this end, a list of useful references has been included in Annex C. These could form the core of a basic technical library.

(ii) In some cases it may be necessary for project staff to contract in or otherwise out-source specialist assistance as and when required. Provision for this needs to be built-in to the project's design.

13.3.2 Opportunities and willingness to engage with users

If at all possible engineers should be involved in participatory exercises used to identify people's preferences. This helps ensure that questions of clarification or substance are addressed and are not overlooked. Later on in the project, engineers may need to engage with users to develop options, facilitate decision making and even to negotiate demand taking into account the capacity and resources available.

Dialogue may involve a number of communication techniques tailored for a specific target audience (see Section 10.3.2). Applying these techniques effectively may require a skilled intermediary.

Engineers should therefore be able and willing to *work alongside* social facilitators in the field, and work *with* rather than *in* communities, using a range of appropriate tools and techniques.

If working with communities is difficult, working with the poor is that much harder. Physically this often requires an arduous walk of several hours and, in some cases, several days. It may mean operating in environments where personal security or health can be major concerns.

More fundamentally, working with vulnerable groups demands a degree of respect for cultures, social status or lifestyles that few engineers have experienced. It often calls for considerable patience and an ability to listen. It may be necessary to meet on a weekend in the late afternoon. Apart from having sufficient time and access to transport, a certain attitude of mind is needed to engage in this way, reinforced by adequate incentives.

13.3.3 Ability to cost options

As already implied, costing options (see Section 10.4) is an integral part of the project process and an important responsibility for engineers, especially in the absence of a financial adviser. Accuracy is needed if the results are used, directly or indirectly, to set user charges.

The research conducted during the preparation of these guidelines suggests that relatively few engineers have the knowledge and skills to do this. In particular, *replacement costs* are frequently over looked, even for facilities with a relatively short life-span such as a communal hand pump. Depending on the project's financial policy, additional training may be required by engineers to ensure that replacement costs are reflected in the prices charged.

13.3.4 Ability and willingness to adapt standards

Depending on the local situation, standard designs and specifications will often have to be adapted to suit user demands, taking into account the safety of users and environmental health risks.

Engineers are often reluctant to adapt standard designs because it contradicts their professional training and may lead to problems with the relevant technical authority. As well as this, engineers may not be entirely confident to design a customised or 'made to measure' solution. Adapting a standard design increases the amount of work required - with cost implications.

As long as the result is relatively safe and cost effective, adapting a standard design or specification to improve its effectiveness and sustainability can be justified. Ideally, engineers should be able to assess each situation from a risk-based perspective, taking into account the potentially negative effect of imposing an inappropriate standard. For example, Argoss (2001) describes how the relative risk of groundwater pollution caused by on-site sanitation can be measured.

A example illustrating the need to adapt a standard design is illustrated in Box 13.1. This concerns the provision of a public latrine block in a market in Tanzania.

Box 13.1. Adapting standard designs to meet demand

The importance of adapting rather than applying a standard design is demonstrated in an example from a peri-urban town in Tanzania. This concerns the provision of a public latrine in a newly developed market place. A standard four-cubicle toilet block had been built, consisting of four cubicles (two for men, two for women) and a male urinal. Even before the latrine block was opened to the public, a number of potential problems were apparent:

- the majority of people in the market were women, but the level of service offered was biased in favour of male users;

- women may not be comfortable using a toilet facility shared (and in this case, managed) by men;

- no provision had been made for hand washing;

- the VIP sanitation technology used may not be acceptable to Muslims who made up a significant proportion of the local population.

As the toilet had not been opened at the time of the visit, it is fair to say that these points are based on assumption rather than evidence. In this case, it would have been relatively easy to adapt the standard design, taking into account user perceptions, enhancing its potential impact and sustainability.

Deverill and Wedgwood (2001)

13.3.5 Ability to provide mixed service levels

Few engineers used to a supply-led environment will be familiar with the provision of mixed levels of service and the implications this has for management[28]. The introduction of mixed service levels can significantly increase the complexity of managing a project, especially if it involves a piped water supply.

---

[28] For example, Bos (2000) established that fewer than 15% of South African water supply engineers she interviewed during the course of her research had ever provided more than communal standpipes for rural users.

In such circumstances, the introduction of mixed service levels should be carefully considered, taking into account the issues identified in Section 10 in these guidelines.

Assuming resources are available, the most important point is to respect collective preferences. *Higher service levels should never be imposed* simply because they are considered to be a visible 'indicator' of a demand responsive approach. In many cases, collective demand for an equitable basic level of service may have to be satisfied first before people are willing to investigate the possibility of offering higher levels of service. In such circumstances, engineers may be expected to suggest solutions designed to help local managers cope with unmet individual demands.

13.4 Summary: knowledge, skills and attitudes

The points raised above emphasise that engineers are likely to be more effective if they can demonstrate the following core qualities:

- A thorough knowledge of a broad range of technologies, associated management and contribution systems, their potential advantages and disadvantages.

- Technical skills, for example, those needed to match the attributes of what is required with technological solutions and to cost options.

- Communication skills to engage and consult with potential users including women and the poor.

- Attitudes that respect and promote the participation of all users in the project process, including women and the poor.

- An ability to work as a member of a project team, respecting the contributions made by other professions.

Table 13.1 identifies these qualities in more detail, and could be adapted by a project manager to help recruit or assess engineering staff. One further point should be recognised: engineers may want to engage in a demand responsive approach, but may need support in order to do so effectively. In fact, the same may apply to all the staff involved. This suggests that it may be useful to introduce a demand responsive approach incrementally and pilot it before scaling it up. Its potential benefits can then be balanced with the capacity to implement and support it. This issue is one of several discussed in Book 2 of these guidelines *Additional Notes for Policy Makers and Planners.*

Table 13.1.	Knowledge, skills and attitudes of engineers needed to design to meet demand. This list is indicative: in practice what is required depends on the local context	
Knowledge	**Skills**	**Attitudes**
Knowledge of policies, legislation and institutional arrangements which influence technical decisions.	Ability to adapt technologies to meet demand, providing mixed levels of service and upgradable systems.	Ability to work as part of a multidisciplinary project team - without necessarily leading it.
Knowledge of individual and team roles and responsibilities and of key working relationships.	Ability to cost options and recommend prices based on the results of demand assessment.	Willingness and patience to devolve decision making to communities and households.
Knowledge of a range of water supply and sanitation options, their flexibility and limitations.	Ability to communicate technical (and possibly financial) concepts to people with little or no technical background.	Willingness to work unconventional hours and to work in remote or difficult situations.
Knowledge of how to cost options accurately.	Ability to negotiate demand taking into account resource and environmental constraints.	Willingness to adapt standards as appropriate, assessing risk and retaining technical responsibility.
Knowledge of technical standards, their basis and adaptability.		
Knowledge of a range of management options and contribution systems.	Ability to engage with all users, especially the poor and women.	Sensitivity to the demands, culture and circumstances of vulnerable groups, especially women and the poor.
Knowledge of wider applications of water and environmental sanitation (e.g. small-scale irrigation, sustainable urban drainage and garbage disposal).	Ability to train local managers, implementers and support staff in technical, managerial and financial skills.	Willingness to improve personal knowledge and skills as part of continuous professional education.
Knowledge of a number of participatory techniques, their use and limitations, and how to apply them.		Willingness to support the project team by improving basic technical knowledge and skills.

References

References

ARGOSS (2001) *Guidelines for Assessing the Risk to Groundwater from On-Site Sanitation*, 2001, British Geological Survey Commissioned Report CR/01/142. NERC Wallingford, Oxfordshire (UK) 2001.

Bajracharya, D. and Deverill, P. (2001) 'NEWAH: Developing a Poverty focused, Demand Responsive Approach.' Paper presented at 27th WEDC conference. Lusaka, August 20th - 24th, 2001.

Breslin, N (2000a) *'Lessons from the field - update series: Maúa and Nipepe'*. Update Number 5, May 2000. Emailed report available from p.a.deverill@lboro.ac.uk

Breslin, N (2000b) *'Lessons from the field - update series: Maúa and Nipepe'*. Update Number 8, September 2000. Emailed report available from p.a.deverill@lboro.ac.uk

Bos, A. (2000) *The role of engineers in the damand responsive approach - a study from South Africa*. A WEDC MSc demand study in International Development. Water, Engineering and Development Centre, UK

Cairncross, S. (1992) *Sanitation and Water Supply: Practical Lessons from the Decade: Water and Sanitation*. Discussion Paper Series No 9. Water and Sanitation Programme Washington DC, 1992

Concern Worldwide (2000) Mtwara CDS *Programme: an Assessment of the Implementation of Demand Responsive Approach in the Community Development Support Programme*. Final Report. Quest Consult, Dar es Salaam, April 2000

Deverill, P. and Wedgwood, A. (2001) *Designing Water Supply and Sanitation Projects to Meet Demand - Reports from field visits to: South Africa, Tanzania, Nepal and India*. WEDC May 2001.

DFID (2000) *Realising Human Rights for Poor People - Strategies for Achieving the International Development Targets*. DFID, London, October 2000.

EHP (1997) *Better Sanitation Programming: a UNICEF handbook.* UNICEF April 1997. http://www.ehproject.org

ERM (2002) *Cost Recovery in Water and Sanitation Projects* Draft Final Position Report. ERM Reference 6278, London, March 2002.

Gosling, L and Matthews, M. (1995) *Toolkits: A Practical Guide to Assessment, Monitoring, Review and Evaluation.* ISBN 1 870322 93 2. Save the Children Fund (UK), London, 1995

GTZ (1995) *Gender Sensitive Participatory Approaches in Technical Co-operation: a Trainer's Manual for Local Experts* Deutsche Gesellschaft für Technishe Zusammenarbeit Eschborn, 1995

Hausermann, J. (1999) *A Human Rights Approach to Development - Some Practical Implications for WaterAid's Work,* 1st WaterAid Lecture, 10th September 1999. WaterAid, London, 1999

Howard, Guy (2002) *Water quality surveillance - a practical guide.* WEDC

IIED (1992) *RRA Notes Number 15* Special Issue on Applications of Wealth Ranking. IIED Sustainable Agriculture Programme, London, May 1992

IRC (1997) *Linking Technology Choice with Operation and Maintenance for Low Cost Water Supply and Sanitation.* Operation and Maintenance Working Group of Water Supply and Sanitation Collaborative Council. IRC, the Netherlands, 1997

Leblanc, M.E. (2001) *The Integration of water supply and sanitation: a success?* MSc Research Project, Water, Engineering and Development Centre, WEDC (2001)

MacGranahan G. Leitman, J. Surjadi, C. (1997) *Understanding Environmental Problems in Disadvantaged Neighbourhoods: Broad Spectrum Surveys, Participatory Appraisal and Contingent Valuation.* Urban Management Programme Working Paper 16. Stockholm Environment Institute, 1997

Mukherjee, Neela (2001) *Achieving Sustained Sanitation for the Poor Policy and Strategy Less from Participatory Assessments in Cambodia, Indonesia, Vietnam.* Water and Sanitation Program (East Asia and the Pacific) april 2001.

Mukherjee, Neela (1992) 'Villager's Perceptions of Rural Poverty through the Mapping Methods of PRA'. Pp 21-26, *RRA Notes Number 15 Special Issue on Applications of Wealth Ranking.* IIED Sustainable Agriculture Programme. London, May 1992

Mvula Trust (1996) *Specific Policies for Water and Sanitation Project Development.* Version 7. Mvula Trust, Braamfontein, South Africa, November 1996.

Ndezi, T. and Wedgwood, A. (2001) 'Assessing Demand in Peri-urban Areas of Dar es Salaam'. Paper presented at 27th WEDC conference. Lusaka, August 20th - 24th, 2001.

Netshiswinzhe, B. and Potter, A. (2000) *Developing Community-based Monitoring and Evaluation Tools for Rural Water and Sanitation Projects* Final Report. Mvula Trust, Johannesburg, November 2000

Ockelford, J. and Reed, R. (2000) *Guidelines for Planning and Designing Rural Water Supply and Sanitation Programmes.* DFID KaR Output. WEDC, June 2000

Sansom, K. Coates, S. Njiru, C. and Franceys, R. (2000) *Strategic Marketing to Improve Water Utility Finances and Services to Poor Urban Water Consumers.* WEDC discussion paper. WEDC, June 2000

Tipping, J and Scott, R. (2001) 'Piloting Trickle-Feed Distribution in Rural South Africa' Paper presented at 27th WEDC conference. Lusaka, August 20th - 24th, 2001.

Toot, M. (2000) Presentation on Kenya/Netherlands Rural Water Supply and Sanitation Development Project, to WEDC, September 2000.

WaterAid (2001) *Looking Back: the Long-term Impacts of Water and Sanitation Projects.* Condensed Report, WaterAid, London, June 2001

Wedgwood, A. and Sansom, K (2001) *Willingness-to-pay surveys - A streamlined approach - guidance notes for small town water services.* Initial draft. Water Engineers and Development Centre October 2001. www.lboro.ac.uk/wedc/projects/omnwss

WEDC (forthcoming) *Infrastructure for All.* A practical guide for engineers, technicians and project managers on how they can meet the needs of men and women in development projects (expected to be published in early 2002) Project website: www.lboro.ac.uk/wedc/projects/msgender/index

WELL (1998) DFID *Guidance Manual on Water Supply and Sanitation Programmes.* WELL, 1998

Whittington, D. Davis, J. and McClelland, E. (1998) 'Implementing a Demand-driven Approach to Community Water Supply Planning: a Case Study of Lugazi, Uganda' *Water International*, Vol. 23, pages 134-145

WHO (2000) Global Water Supply and Sanitation Assessment 2000. WHO, Geneva, Switzerland. Details at:
http://www.who.int/water_sanitation_health/Globassessment/Global1.htm

World Bank (1993) 'The demand for water in rural areas: determinants and policy implications' *World Bank Water Demand Research Team Observer,* pages 47-70, Volume 8 no. 1, January 1993

Glossary

Glossary

Affordability	The capacity to pay for a service. Affordability is often *assumed* by project staff, based on a fixed proportion of household income or the ownership of assets rather than on user perceptions of the service on offer.
Amortization	A method of calculating the amount of money needed to be set aside each year theannuity to replace equipment at the end of its expected operational life.
Bidding game	A method of establishing the maximum amount an individual is willing to pay for a specified service. The technique is often used in contingent valuation.
Coping strategy	A behaviour or practice used to sustain or improve a livelihood. See also Revealed Preference.
Contingent valuation	A demand assessment technique. Several options (each associated with a range of prices) are described to a sample of potential users who then indicate their preferences. The technique requires specialist skills and is most cost effective in high-density urban and peri-urban areas.
Demand	Demand is defined in these guidelines as: *an informed expression of desire for a particular service, assessed by the investments people are prepared to make, over the lifetime of the service, to receive and sustain it.*
Demand assessment	Any technique used to gauge or measure demand. These can be classified as (i) indirect, based mostly on field observations (e.g. a revealed preference survey), or (ii) direct, relying on people expressing an opinion about a particular service (as used in contingent valuation).

Demand stimulation	Techniques used to unlock latent demand. This may involve promoting the characteristics of options which are known to be desirable. This reinforces the importance of developing options that take into account people's preferences and priorities.
Economy of scale	If an option becomes more cost effective when applied on a larger scale, it is said to exhibit an economy of scale. However, larger projects are not necessarily more cost effective than smaller ones, because they may require more complex (and more expensive) solutions.
Effective demand	Demand for a good or service expressed by a user's willingness to pay in terms of a monetary or economic contribution.
Enabling enviroment	Relevant policies, legislation and institutional arrangements that support the design and implementation of projects and the sustainability of the services provided.
Felt need	An immediate necessity, as perceived by the individual or household concerned. A felt need becomes a demand if it is supported by a commitment to invest resources, interest or time to receive and sustain it.
Focus group	A small group of individuals with a similar social, cultural or economic background, brought together with a facilitator to explore a particular issue.
Harijan	A low caste community, family or individual in Hindu culture.
Latent demand	Demand which is only revealed after it has been stimulated. See demand stimulation.
Livelihood	The capacity, assets (a combination of social, human, financial, natural and physical resources) and activities needed to sustain a particular life style.

PHAST	*Participatory Hygiene and Sanitation Transformation*: a technique that encourages group learning and understanding of links between hygiene and sanitation, based on the use of mainly graphical tools.
Positive deviance	Behaviour or practice which have positive impact in terms of environmental health but which deviates from established norms.
PREPP	*Participation, Ranking, Experience, Perceptions and Partnership:* A recently developed demand assessment technique employing components of contingent valuation in a focus group discussion.
Revealed preference survey	A socio-economic survey of people's coping strategies used by economists to assess demand for an existing or planned service.
Sanitation	In its narrowest sense, sanitation is the safe management of human excreta. More broadly, the term includes the management of wastewater, solid waste and storm water drainage.
Service	The system that provides users with a particular function (e.g. improved water supply or sanitation). A service includes facilities and their management, contribution and support mechanisms.
Service level	Used to describe the relative quality of the service being provided to users. This is often associated with physical infrastructure, for example, a communal tap or well, a yard tap or family well, and an in-house private connection.
Social marketing	The application of marketing techniques to stimulate demand. The underlying motivation is to reduce exposure to environmental health risks rather than a profit motive.

<u>Sustainable livelihoods</u>	A holistic approach to development, focusing on people's assess to and control over assets and resources; their vulnerability and the supporting framework (made up of policies, legislation and institutions).
<u>Triangulation</u>	Confirming the results of a sociological investigation by cross checking with the results of other investigations.
<u>Want</u>	A desire for a good or service that goes beyond a felt need in that it may satisfy a person's longer term needs or aspirations.
<u>Water demand</u>	The quantity of water people use or are expected to use. As such water demand is an important technical design parameter.
<u>Willingness to pay</u>	The financial or economic contribution that people are willing to make to receive and sustain a particular service. See effective demand and contingent valuation.

Annexes

Value of Annuity Factors AF(r,n) at interest rate r% running for n years

AF(r,n) = [1-(1+r)^(-n)] / r	Annuity = Current Value / AF(r,n)

No of years (n)	Interest Rate (r)							
	3%	5%	6%	8%	10%	12%	15%	20%
1	0.9709	0.9524	0.9434	0.9259	0.9091	0.8929	0.8696	0.8111
2	1.9135	1.8594	1.8334	1.7833	1.7355	1.6901	1.6257	1.4726
3	2.8286	2.7232	2.6730	2.5771	2.4869	2.4018	2.2832	2.0146
4	3.7171	3.5460	3.4651	3.3121	3.1699	3.0373	2.8550	2.4611
5	4.5797	4.3295	4.2124	3.9927	3.7908	3.6048	3.3522	2.8306
6	5.4172	5.0757	4.9173	4.6229	4.3553	4.1114	3.7845	3.1378
7	6.2303	5.7864	5.5824	5.2064	4.8684	4.5638	4.1604	3.3944
8	7.0197	6.4632	6.2098	5.7466	5.3349	4.9676	4.4873	3.6096
9	7.7861	7.1078	6.8017	6.2469	5.7590	5.3282	4.7716	3.7909
10	8.5302	7.7217	7.3601	6.7101	6.1446	5.6502	5.0188	3.9443
11	9.2526	8.3064	7.8869	7.1390	6.4951	5.9377	5.2337	4.0746
12	9.9540	8.8633	8.3838	7.5361	6.8137	6.1944	5.4206	4.1857
13	10.6350	9.3936	8.8527	7.9038	7.1034	6.4235	5.5831	4.2807
14	11.2961	9.8986	9.2950	8.2442	7.3667	6.6282	5.7245	4.3624
15	11.9379	10.3797	9.7122	8.5595	7.6061	6.8109	5.8474	4.4328
20	14.8775	12.4622	11.4699	9.8181	8.5136	7.4694	6.2593	4.6681
22	15.9369	13.1630	12.0416	10.2007	8.7715	7.6446	6.3587	4.7264
25	17.4131	14.0939	12.7834	10.6748	9.0770	7.8431	6.4641	4.7910
30	19.6004	15.3725	13.7648	11.2578	9.4269	8.0552	6.5660	4.8597

Keep it up?

YES ← **Is the amount of money collected enough to cover the running costs of the project?** → **NO**

If no, the committee could take the following actions:
- Cut off water
- Fine defaulters
- Give warning
- Report to community
- Report to traditional leaders

If no, how were the costs recovered:
- Through savings

  Amount

- Other (explain) _____

  Amount

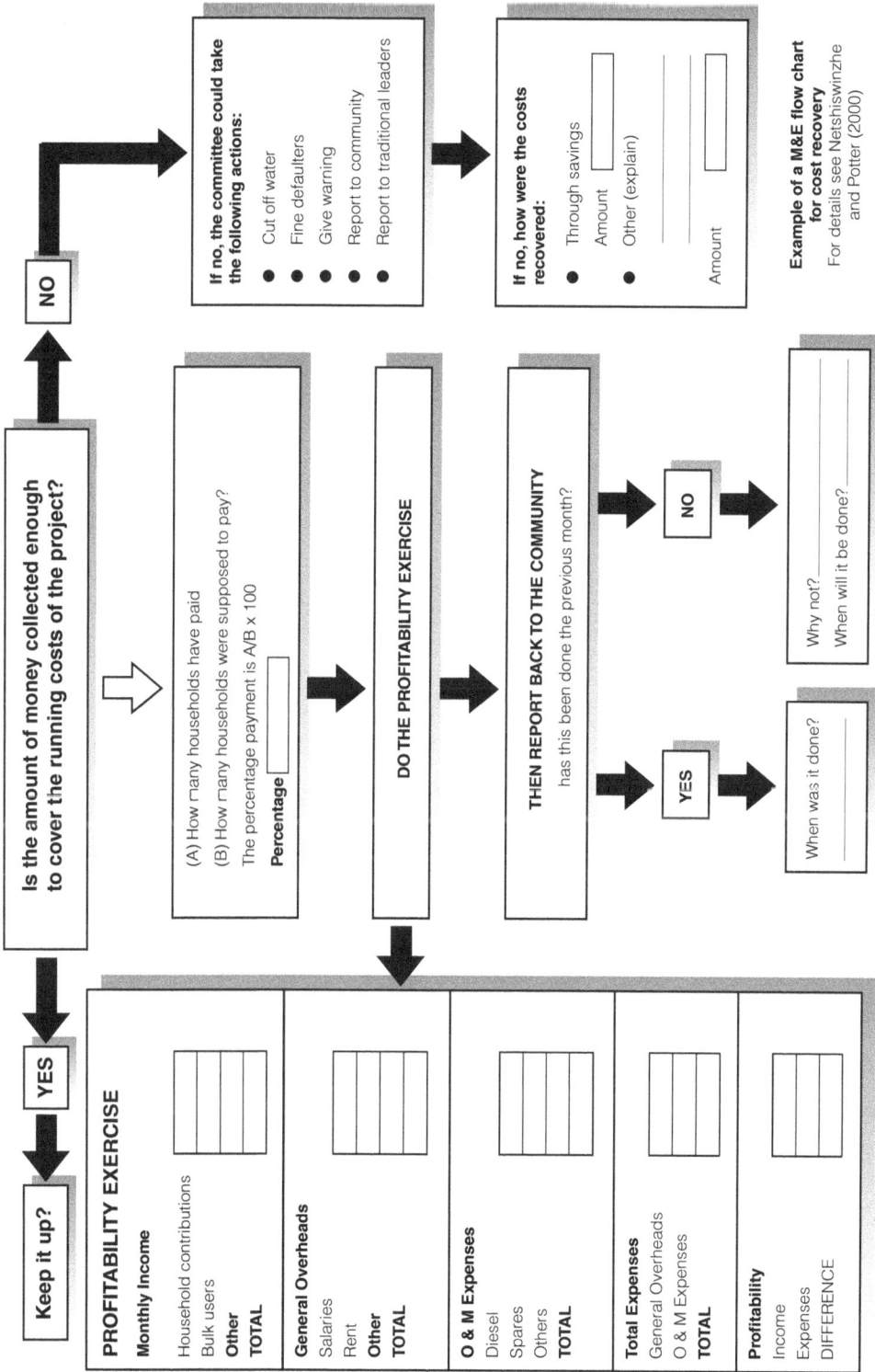

Example of a M&E flow chart for cost recovery
For details see Netshiswinzhe and Potter (2000)

(A) How many households have paid
(B) How many households were supposed to pay?
The percentage payment is A/B x 100

Percentage [ ]

DO THE PROFITABILITY EXERCISE

THEN REPORT BACK TO THE COMMUNITY
has this been done the previous month?

YES → When was it done? _____

NO → Why not? _____
When will it be done? _____

PROFITABILITY EXERCISE

Monthly Income
Household contributions
Bulk users
Other
TOTAL

General Overheads
Salaries
Rent
Other
TOTAL

O & M Expenses
Diesel
Spares
Others
TOTAL

Total Expenses
General Overheads
O & M Expenses
TOTAL

Profitability
Income
Expenses
DIFFERENCE

Project Name:

Completed by:

For the period:

District:

Date	Problem reported and located	Action taken	Review of action taken to fix problem			Comments
			Is the problem fixed (Yes/No)	If yes, date fixed	If no, what action will or has been taken to fix the problem?	

Example of an M&E Logsheet

For details see Netshiswinzhe and Potter (2000)

Suggested reference books

Below is a short list of books and publications that the authors consider to be most useful for engineers and project technical staff, taking into account their roles and responsibilities in designing to meet demand.

Water supply and sanitation

The Worth of Water: Technical briefs on health, water and sanitation by Rod Shaw, edited by John Pickford. 132 pages. ISBN 1 85339 069 0.

■ Published by Intermediate Technology Publications, 103-105 Southampton Row, London, WC1B 4HH, UK. http://www.developmentbookshop.com

■ A series of short, illustrated introductions to the main technologies and process in village and community level water and sanitation.

Running Water: More technical briefs for health, water and sanitation by Rod Shaw, introduced by Ian Smout. 128 pages. ISBN 1 85339450 5

■ Published by Intermediate Technology Publications, 103-105 Southampton Row, London, WC1B 4HH, UK. http://www.developmentbookshop.com

■ This second collection of 32 short, illustrated introductions to appropriate water and sanitation technologies and processes complements *The Worth of Water*. It covers a further range of subjects from water source selection and handpump maintenance to sanitary surveying, hygiene understanding and community management.

Sanitation

Low-cost Sanitation: A survey of practical experience by John Pickford. 167 pages. ISBN 1 85339 233 2.

■ Published in 1997 by Intermediate Technology Publications, 103-105 Southampton Row, London, WC1B 4HH, UK. http://www.developmentbookshop.com

- A guide to what has been learnt about providing sanitation for rural and urban low income communities, outlining what is appropriate, practical and acceptable. Includes an examination of the health, social and economic aspects of sanitation in different parts of the world.

A guide to the development of on-site sanitation by Richard Franceys, John Pickford and Bob Reed of the Water, Engineering and Development Centre. 237 pages. ISBN 92 4 15443 0

- Published in 1992 by the World Health Organisation: Distribution and Sales, World Health Organisation, 1211 Geneva,27, Switzerland

- In-depth technical information about the design, construction, operation and maintenance of the major types of on-site sanitation facility, from simple pit latrines to aqua privies and septic tanks.

Latrine Building : A handbook for implementation of the SanPlat system by Björn Brandberg. 168 pages. ISBN 1 85339306 1

- Published in 1997 by Intermediate Technology Publications, 103-105 Southampton Row, London, WC1B 4HH, UK. http://www.developmentbookshop.com

- Describes the Sanplat system for building improved latrines. The book describes in detail how to make SanPlats and how to implement a latrine building programme, including hygiene education.

Water supply
Small Community Water Supplies: Technology of Small Water Supply Systems in Developing Countries IRC Technical Paper 18. Compiled and edited by E.H.Hofkes. 442 pages. ISBN 0 471 90289 6.

- Current edition published in 1983 by the IRC. Order reference TP-18. International Water and Sanitation Centre, PO Box 2869, 2601 Delft, the Netherlands. http://www.irc.nl

- A core handbook designed as a broad introduction into the technology of small water supply systems in developing countries. Targeted at engineers and technical staff involved in Water Supply programmes and projects.

Making your water supply work: Operation and Maintenance of small water supplies Occasional Paper no 29 by Jan Davis and François Brikké. 108 pages.

■ Published in 1995 by the IRC International Water and Sanitation Centre. Order reference OP29-E. Available as a free pdf file from the IRC website. IRC International Water and Sanitation Centre, PO Box 2869, 2601 Delft, the Netherlands. http://www.irc.nl

■ Recent experience on trends and developments in the operation and maintenance of water supply systems of small communities, based on a review of available literature and the field experience of the authors. Describes O&M systems for a number of low cost technologies.

Rainwater Catchment Systems for Domestic Water Supply: Design, construction and implementation by John Gould and Erik Nissen-Pietersen. 335 pages. ISBN 1 85 339456 4.

■ Published in 1999 by Intermediate Technology Publications, 103-105 Southampton Row, London, WC1B 4HH, UK. http://www.developmentbookshop.com

■ A state of the art review of practice in the collection of rainwater to use or supplement household water requirements. All aspects of design are covered, including non-technical as well as technical factors.

Handpumps: Issues and concepts in rural water supply programmes. 163pages ISBN 90-6687-010-9. Written and produced by IRC.

■ Current edition published in 1996 by the IRC International Water and Sanitation Centre. IRC International Water and Sanitation Centre, PO Box 2869, 2601 Delft, the Netherlands. http://www.irc.nl

■ An up-to-date guide covering the application of handpump technology to small community water supplies, from project preparation to operation and maintenance.

A handbook of Gravity-Flow Water Systems by Thomas D. Jordan Jnr.
ISBN 0946688 50 8

■ Reprinted in 2000 by Intermediate Technology Publications, 103-105
Southampton Row, London, WC1B 4HH, UK http://
www.developmentbookshop.com

■ A practical handbook covering all aspects of gravity water supply, from
source selection to pipe line operation.

www.ingramcontent.com/pod-product-compliance
Lightning Source LLC
Chambersburg PA
CBHW051555030426
42334CB00034B/3451